Practical Guide to the Operational Use of the M2 BMG Machine Gun

By Erik Lawrence

Copyright ©2014 Erik Lawrence

Erik Lawrence
www.vig-sec.com   erik@vig-sec.com

Printed and bound in the United States of America

First printing 2008
Second printing 2014

ISBN-10: 1-941998-13-5
ISBN-13: 978-1-941998-13-7
EBOOK – ISBN-13: 978-1-941998-32-8

LCCN: Not Yet Assigned

ATTENTION US MILITARY UNITS, US GOVERNMENT AGENCIES AND PROFESSIONAL ORGANIZATIONS: Quantity discounts are available on bulk purchases of this book. Special books or book excerpts can also be created to fit specific needs. For information, please contact:

Erik Lawrence
www.vig-sec.com   erik@vig-sec.com

SAFETY NOTICE
Before starting an inspection, ensure the weapon is cleared. Do not manipulate the trigger system until the weapon has been cleared of all ammunition. Inspect the chamber to ensure that it is empty and no ammunition is present. Keep the weapon oriented in a safe direction when loading and handling.

AMMUNITION NOTICE - This weapon fires the 12.7x99mm (U.S. .50 BMG), not the 12.7x108mm Soviet. Firing the incorrect ammunition will damage the weapon and possibly injure the operator/assistant operator.

Training should be received from knowledgeable and experienced operators on this particular weapons system. Vigilant Security Services, LCC Training provides this training and continually perfects its instruction with up-to-date information from actual use.

www.vig-sec.com

PREFACE

This manual is intended to be a reference for those involved in the use, maintenance and instruction of the featured firearm. My aim in writing these manuals is to set the record straight and dispel many of the false assumptions related to the different firearms. The early sections of the manual contain background material on the featured firearm which allows the user to gain the basic building blocks for further education. The firearms featured in these manuals have been used for decades by our allies and enemies, and will be for the foreseeable future, so why are we not experts with them? If I am fighting with the firearm or providing instruction on a firearm, I want to use and know their system better than they do.

The rationale for writing these manuals comes from the fact that there are not libraries of easily accessible references to use in developing your own training system for these firearms. Many of the old military field manuals are decades old and were incorrectly translated by someone who had no idea what the firearm could do, let alone basic firearm knowledge. We started from the ground up and developed the manuals to provide instruction in progressive steps that could be easily grasped and continually referred back to. A good grounding in the basics of firearms, safety, and instruction allows the user to use these manuals to their maximum value. A competent user will find little difficulty in interpreting and applying the information in the manual to their own training program.

The guide goes through the most fundamental parts of the firearm in detail and more advanced techniques are not covered as extensively. With this in mind the user can use these principles and adapt it as needed to their required level of instruction. The emphasis of this guide is in acquiring familiarity with the fundamentals of all firearms and learned competence rather than becoming a firearms guru.

Many of the points in these guides were developed from scratch in theatres of conflict and are continually improved and updated for each edition. I have continually used vetted points from users and professionals in the guides to continually update them to the best known practices for each particular firearm. If it is valid and relevant we will include it in the next edition.

Please note that this guide assumes some familiarity with the basic concepts in firearm safety, gun handling skills, common sense and an ability to process new information. Readers should have knowledge of the difference in calibers, countries of origin, and the knowledge of the priority of the skills needed for development.

I hope you find this work useful and remember that a manual does not replace proper training and hands on experience. Please email comments to erik@vig-sec.com, particularly if you find any errors or glaring omissions.

Erik Lawrence

Table of Contents

M2 Browning
.50 Caliber
Heavy Machine Gun

Section 1

Introduction

The objective of this manual is to allow the reader to be able to use competently the Browning M2 .50 caliber weapon system. The manual will give the reader background/specifications of the weapon and instruct on its operation, disassembly and assembly, proper firing procedure, and malfunction/misfire procedures. Operator level maintenance will also be detailed to allow the reader to understand fully and become competent in the use and maintenance of the Browning M2 machine gun.

Using a round originally designed by Winchester, the .50 BMG round was designed as a response to the German 13mm anti-tank rifles of World War I and employed in a redesigned and scaled-up M1917 Browning .30 caliber machine gun. It was quickly adapted to the anti-aircraft role. It was also selected for the ground role and adopted by the U.S. as the Model 1921. The latter served during the 1920s as an anti-aircraft and anti-armor gun. In 1932, the design was updated and adopted as the M2, though carrying out the same functions. With the addition of a thicker-walled barrel for better cooling (though counter-intuitive, a thicker barrel has a larger surface area, and so provides better air-cooling) it became the M2HB (for *Heavy Barrel*). Due to the long procedure for changing the barrel, an improved system was developed called QCB (quick-change barrel). A lightweight version, weighing 24 lb (11 kg) less—a mere 60 lb (27 kg)—was also developed. Variants of the original are still being used by the branches of the U.S. military on tanks and small water craft.

Description

The Browning machine gun (BMG) caliber .50 HB, M2 is a belt-fed, recoil-operated, air-cooled, crew-served machine gun (Figure 1-1). The gun is capable of single shot, as well as automatic fire, and operates on the short recoil principle.

Technical Data

Weight (approx.)	84 pounds
Weight of barrel	24 pounds
Length of gun	65.13 inches
Length of barrel	45 inches
Length of rifling (approx.)	41.88 inches
Number of lands and grooves	8
Twist, right-hand	one turn in 15 inches
Feed	link-belt
Operation	recoil
Cooling	air

Muzzle velocity (approx.)	3,050 feet per second
Rate of fire (cyclic)	450 to 550 rounds per minute
Maximum range (approx.)	7,440 yards or 6,764 meters
Maximum effective range	(approx.) 2,000 yards or 1,830 meters
• Area targets	1,830 meters
• Point targets, single shot	1,500 meters

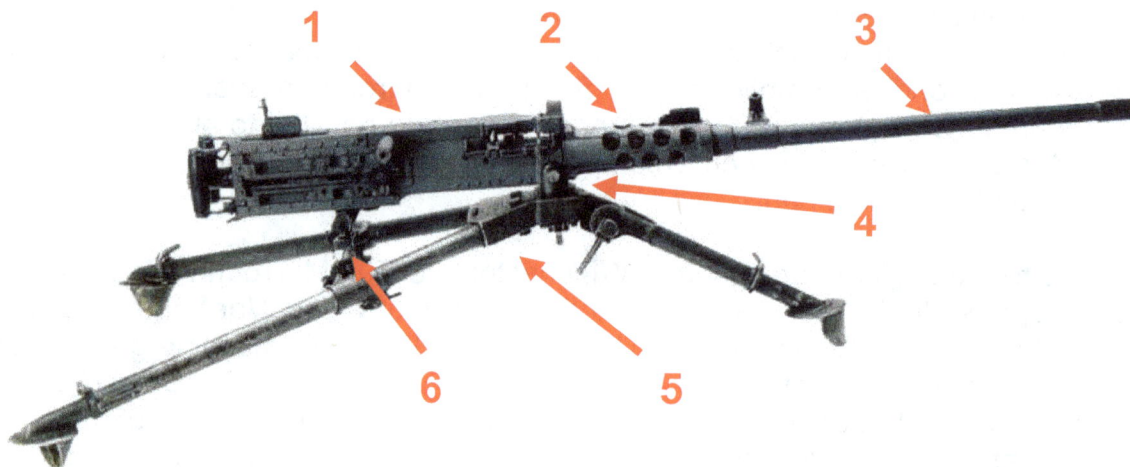

Figure 1-1 M2 .50 BMG on M3 Tripod

1- Receiver
2- Barrel Support
3- Barrel Group
4- Pintle
5- Tripod Mount, M3
6- Traversing and Elevating Mechanism

The BMG is the most successful design of its time.

The machine gun is capable of being fed from either the right or left by repositioning certain parts. The weapon has non-fixed headspace that must be set. Timing must also be adjusted to cause the gun to fire slightly out of battery to prevent damage to moving parts. The force for recoil operation is furnished by expanding powder gases, which are controlled by various springs, cams, and levers. Maximum surface of the barrel and receiver are exposed to permit air cooling. Perforations in the barrel support allow air to circulate around the breach end of the barrel and help in cooling the parts. A heavy barrel is used to retard early overheating.

The gun has a leaf-type rear sight (Figure 1-2a), graduated in both yards and mils. The scale ranges from 100 to 2,600 in yards, and from 0 to 62 in mils. The windage knob permits deflection changes to right or left of center. The front sight is a fixed-blade type with cover (Figure 1-2b).

Figure 1-2a Rear Tangent Sight

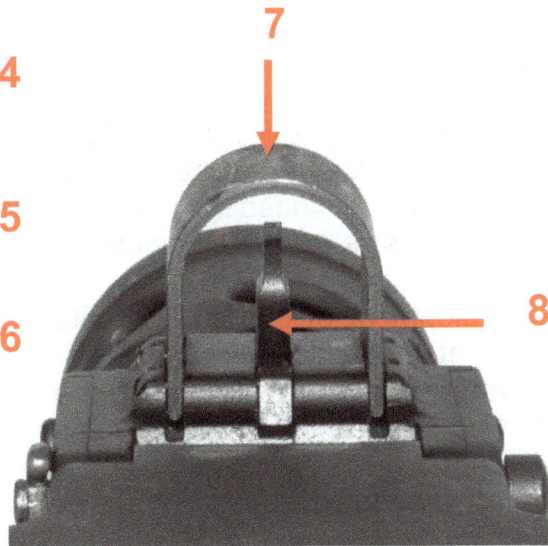

Figure 1-2b Front Sight

1 – Windage Knob
2 – Mils
3 – Range in Yards and Mils
4 – Elevating Screw Knob

5 – Yards
6 – Deflection in Mils
7 – Cover
8 – Blade

Combat Usage

The M2 .50 Browning machine gun is used for various roles:
- A medium infantry support weapon.
- When doubled, it is used as an anti-aircraft gun in some ships, or on the ground. In these cases, a pair of one left-handed and one right-handed feeds are used. In some cases, four to six guns are mounted on the turret.
- Primary or secondary weapon on an armored fighting vehicle.
- Primary or secondary weapon on a naval patrol boat.
- Secondary weapon for anti-boat defense on naval destroyers, frigates, and aircraft carriers.
- Coaxial gun or independent mounting in some tanks.
- A primary armament in WWII-era U.S. aircraft, such as the P-51 Mustang, and the Korean-era U.S. F-86 Saber.
- Defensive armament in WWII-era bombers like the B-17 Flying Fortress and B-24 Liberators.
- A long-range sniper rifle, when attached with a scope. One well-known expert was U.S. Marine sniper Carlos Hathcock during the Vietnam War. The success of the M2 in this role led to the development of actual sniper rifles based on the same .50 caliber round.
- A water-cooled version of the larger M2 was used as an emplaced or vehicle-mounted anti-aircraft weapon on a sturdy pedestal mount.

M2 Variants

The basic M2 was deployed in U.S. service in a number of sub variants, all with separate complete designations as per the U.S. Army system. The basic designation as mentioned in the introduction is **Browning Machine Gun, Cal. .50, M2**, with others as described below.

The development of the M1921 water-cooled machine gun that led to the M2 meant that the initial M2s were in fact water-cooled. These weapons were designated **Browning Machine Gun, Cal. .50, M2, Water-cooled, Flexible**. There was no fixed water-cooled version.

Improved air-cooled heavy-barrel versions came in three subtypes: the basic infantry model, **Browning Machine Gun, Cal. .50, M2, HB, Flexible**; a fixed developed for use on the M6 Heavy Tank designated **Browning Machine Gun, Cal. .50, M2, HB, Fixed**; and a "turret type" whereby "Flexible" M2s were modified slightly for use in tank turrets. The sub variant designation **Browning Machine Gun, Cal. .50, M2, HB, Turret** was used only for manufacturing, supply, and administration identification and separation from flexible M2s. Specific aircraft versions were also developed, and these sub-variants are discussed in the following paragraph, along with the AN/M2.

AN/M2, M3, XM296/M296, and GAU-10/A

The **M2** machine gun was heavily used as a remote-fired fixed weapon, primarily in aircraft, but also in other applications. For this application a variant of the M2 was developed (sometimes seen under the designation **AN/M2**, but it is important to note that there were .30 and .50 caliber weapons with this designation) with the ability to fire from a solenoid trigger. For aircraft mounting, some were also fitted with substantially lighter barrels, permitted by the cooling effect of air in the slip-stream. The official designation for this weapon was **Browning Machine Gun, Aircraft, Caliber .50, M2,** followed by either "Fixed" or Flexible" depending on whether the weapon was used as a fixed forward firing gun or for use by an airplane's crew, such as a waist-gun position on a B-17.

The **M3** was a more purpose-built variant for remote firing use, which also featured a higher rate of fire.

The **XM296/M296** is a further development of the M2/M3 machine gun for remote firing applications and is currently used in armament systems pertaining to the OH-58 Kiowa Warrior helicopter. The M296 differs from previous remote firing variants primarily in the lack of a bolt latch, allowing for single shots.

The **GAU-10/A** (NSN or National Stock Number 1005-01-029-3428) has been identified as a member of the Browning M2 family through its inclusion in the June 2000 issue of *Countermeasure* (Volume 21, No 6.) *Countermeasure* is published by the Army Ground Risk Management Team and identifies important issues that soldiers should be aware of with regards to risk management and safety. Beyond this connection, there is no specific information on the GAU-10/A, and it is odd that the only online reference would be from a U.S. Army publication as this is a USAF designation.

XM213/M213, XM218, GAU-15/A, GAU-16/A, and GAU-18/A

The **XM213/M213** was a modernization and adaptation of existing .50 caliber **AN/M2s** in inventory for use as a pintle-mounted door gun on helicopters.

The **GAU-16/A** was an improved GAU-15/A with modified grip and sight assemblies for similar applications.

The **GAU-18/A**, formerly identified as the **XM218**, is a lightweight variant of the M2/M3 and is used on the USAF's MH-53J Pave low II and HH-60 Pave Hawk helicopters. These weapons do not utilize the heavy barrel and are typically set up as left-hand feed, right-hand charging weapons. In this configuration, the gun is fitted with a chute adapter attached to its left-hand feed-pawl bracket. Thus, the weapon can receive ammunition through a feed chute system connected to internally mounted ammunition cans. Originally designed to accommodate 1,700 rounds, these cans have since been modified due to space constraints and now hold about half that amount. However, many aerial gunners find the chute system cumbersome and opt to install a bracket accommodating the 100-round cans instead.

GAU-21/A and M3P Variants

Figure 1-3 GAU-21 used on Huey Helicopter

The FN-produced M3 series is also in U.S. military service in two versions, one being a fixed remote-firing version, the **FN M3P**, used on the Avenger Air Defense System. The U.S. Army would appear to use this designation for the weapon.

The M3M is also known as the GAU-21, and is an updated .50 caliber machine gun that's envisioned as the primary suppressive fire system for Navy and Marine

Corps helicopters and V-22 Ospreys (Figure 1-3 & 1-4). In exchange for slightly less range than the older M2, it offers a higher firing rate (1100 rpm vs. 550), lighter weight (80 pounds vs. 128), longer barrel life (11,000 rounds vs. 3,000), better safety (open breech eliminates cook-off), and reduced recoil (by up to 67%, improving accuracy). The GAU-21 can also be converted for dismounted use by one person in 2 minutes.

Figure 1-4 M3M/GAU-21/A Aircraft model

M2E50 (or M2 E-50)

A long-due upgrade program for existing infantry M2s and other M2s currently in U.S. Army service, the E50 finally provides a Quick Change Barrel (QCB) capability, as well as a rail accessory mount, improved flash hider, and a manual safety. While it originally appeared that the E50 was within the bounds of the normal U.S. Army designation system, it is actually a developmental project that stands for Enhanced 50, as in enhanced .50 caliber machine gun. The E50 is a conversion kit that can be applied to older weapons — newer machine guns can be produced to this standard, however.

XM312 Future of the .50 Caliber

Figure 1-5 XM312 .50 Caliber Machine Gun

The **XM312** is a modern heavy machine gun chambered for the 12.7 × 99 mm NATO cartridge which is derived from the XM307 25 mm autocannon (Figure 1-5).

It was designed in response to a request by the US military for a replacement for the aging M2HB heavy machine gun, and as a complement to the heavier XM307. It is expected to be put into service around FY 2008. It is quickly capable of being converted to an XM307 with a small number of parts and a few minutes of work at the unit level (and vice versa from the XM307)

Background

The M2 is a scaled-up version of John Browning's M1917 .30 caliber machine gun (even using the same timing gauges) and fires the .50 BMG cartridge, which today is also used in high-powered sniper rifles and long-range target rifles due to its excellent long-range accuracy, external ballistics performance, incredible stopping power, and lethality. The M2 is an air-cooled, belt-fed machine gun that fires from a closed bolt, operated on the short recoil principle. In this action, the bolt and barrel are initially locked together and recoil upon firing. After a short distance, the bolt and barrel unlock, and the bolt continues to move rearwards relative to the barrel. This action opens the bolt and pulls the belt of ammunition through the weapon, readying it to fire again, all at a cyclic rate of 450-550 rounds per minute. This is a rate of fire not generally achieved in use, as sustained fire at that rate will "shoot out" the barrel within a few thousand rounds, necessitating replacement. The M2 machine gun's sustained rate of fire is considered to be anything less than 40 rounds per minute.

The M2 has a maximum range of 7.4 kilometers (4.2 miles) when using the M2 ball ammunition, with a maximum effective range of 1.8 kilometers (1.2 miles) when fired from the M3 tripod. In its ground-portable, crew-served role, the gun itself weighs in at a hefty 84 pounds (38 kg) and the assembled M3 tripod another 44 pounds (20 kg). In this configuration, the V-shaped trigger is located at the very rear of the weapon, with a "spade handle" hand-grip on either side of it and the bolt release in the center. The "spade handles" are gripped, and the trigger is depressed with one or both thumbs. When the bolt release is in the up position, the weapon is in single-shot mode. The bolt release must be pressed each time the weapon is fired to close the bolt and reload the weapon. The bolt release can be locked into the down position, resulting in fully automatic firing.

Because the M2 was designed with intent in many configurations, it can be adapted to feed in rounds from the left or right side of the weapon by exchanging the belt-holding pawls, the belt-feed pawl, and the front and rear cartridge stops and reversing the bolt switch. The conversion can be completed within a minute with no tools.

When firing blanks, a large blank-firing adapter (BFA) must be used in order to keep the gas pressure high enough to allow the action to cycle. It is very distinctive, attached to the muzzle and the three rods extending back to the base. The BFA can often be seen on M2s in peacetime operations.

International Usage

The M2 family has also been widely used abroad, primarily in its basic infantry configuration. Here is a quick listing of foreign designations for M2- family weapons.

Country	NATO Member	Designation	Description
Australia	No	M2HB	12.7x99mm Browning M2HB machine gun (manufactured locally under license by ADI[1]
Austria	No	üsMG M2	12.7x99mm Browning M2HB machine gun
Belgian Army	Yes	FN M2HB-QCB	12.7x99mm Browning M2HB machine gun, used as infantry weapon, IFV mounted gun and as tank's AA gun
Brazilian Army	No	Mtr .50 M2 HB "BROWNING"	12.7x99mm Browning M2HB machine gun
Canada	Yes	M2	12.7x99mm Browning M2HB machine gun
Chilean Army	No	FN M2HB-QCB	12.7x99mm Browning M2HB machine gun
Denmark	Yes	M/50	12.7x99mm Browning M2HB machine gun
Germany	Yes	MG50-1	12.7x99mm Browning M2HB machine gun
Israel	No	מק"כ ("MAKACH")	12.7x99mm Browning M2HB machine gun, used as infantry weapon, IFV mounted gun and as tank's coaxial gun
Japan	No	12.7 mm M2 (Licensed by Sumitomo Heavy Industries)	12.7x99mm Browning M2HB machine gun, used as IFV-mounted gun and as tank's coaxial gun
South Korea	No	K-6 (Licensed by Daewoo)	12.7x99mm Browning M2HB QCB machine gun
Spain	Yes	Ametralladora Pesada M-2 HB	12.7x99 mm Browning M2HB machine gun
Norway	Yes	M/50	12.7x99mm Browning M2HB machine gun
Sweden	No	Tksp 12,7 (Licensed by Bofors)	12.7x99mm Browning M2HB machine gun

United Kingdom (British Army)	Yes	L2A1	12.7x99mm Browning M2HB machine gun
United Kingdom	Yes	L6, L6A1	12.7x99mm Browning M2 HB machine gun; ranging gun for the L7 105 mm tank gun on the Centurion tank
United Kingdom	Yes	L11, L11A1	12.7x99mm Browning M2HB machine gun; ranging gun
United Kingdom	Yes	L21A1	12.7x99mm Browning M2HB machine gun; ranging gun for the 120mm tank gun on the Chieftain tank
United Kingdom	Yes	L111A1	12.7x99mm Browning/FN M2HB QCB machine gun
Switzerland	No	Mg 64	12.7x99mm Browning M2 HB machine gun

Components

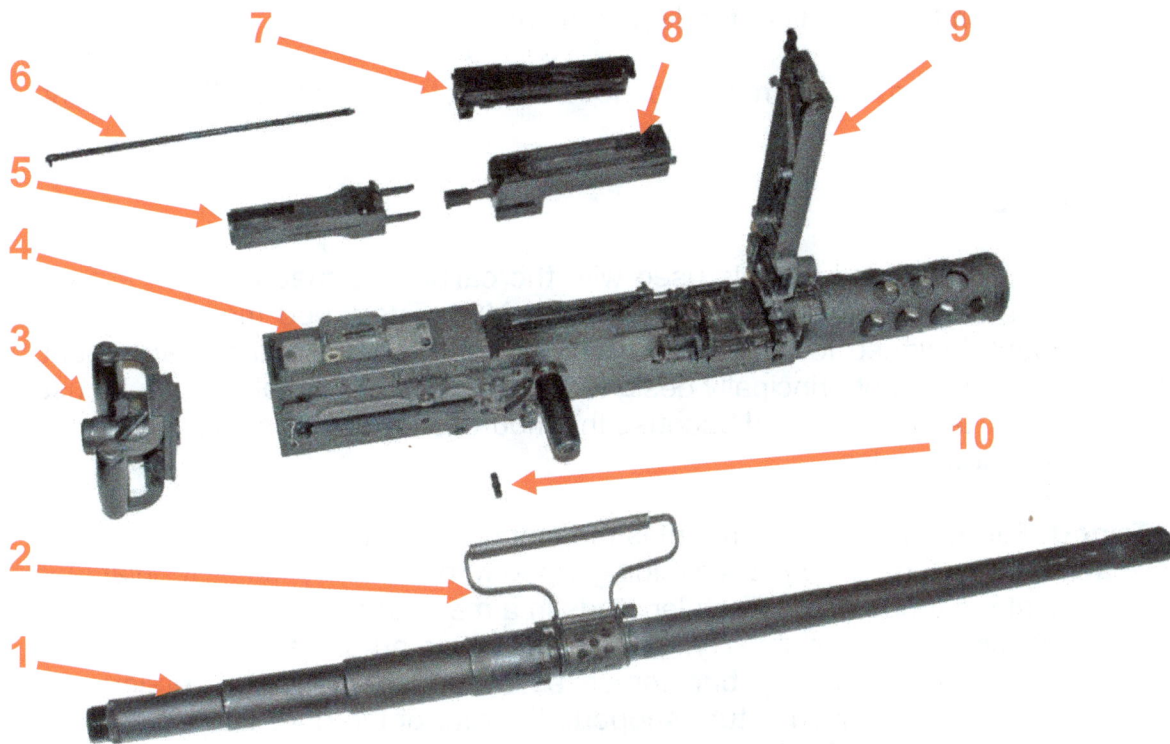

Figure 1-6 Basic components

COMPONENTS AND PURPOSES

1. Barrel Group - Houses cartridges for firing; directs projectile.

2. Carrier Assembly - Provides handle to carry barrel and to remove the barrel from the receiver.

3. Backplate Group - Houses the trigger, bolt latch release, buffer tube sleeve, and the left and right spade grips.

4. Receiver Group - Serves as a support for all major components; houses action of weapon, which controls functioning of weapon.

5. Barrel Buffer Body - Assists in recoil and counter recoil of the bolt group.

6. Driving Spring Rod Assembly - Drives the bolt forward when the bolt latch release is depressed.

7. Bolt Group - Provides feeding, chambering, firing, and extracting, using the propellant gases and recoil spring for power.

8. Barrel Extension Group - Secures the barrel to the recoiling parts.

9. Cover Group - Feeds linked-belt ammunition; positions and holds cartridges in position for extracting, feeding, and chambering.

10. Bolt Stud - Provides a means to move the bolt to the rear with the retracting slide handle.

GROUND MOUNTS

The two principal ground mounts used with the caliber .50 machine gun are the tripod mount, M3, and the anti-aircraft mount, M63. The tripod mount, M3, is a ground mount designed for use against ground targets. The anti-aircraft mount, M63, is a ground mount principally designed for use against aerial targets. Its use against ground targets is limited because the mount tends to be unstable when the gun is fired at low angles.

A. **Tripod Mount, M3.** The M3 mount is the standard ground mount of the caliber .50 machine gun (Figure 1-7). It is a folding tripod with three telescopic tubular legs connected at the tripod head. Each leg ends in a metal shoe that can be stamped into the ground for greater stability. The two trail legs are joined together by the traversing bar. The traversing bar serves as a support for the traversing and elevating mechanism, which in turn supports the rear of the gun. The tripod head furnishes a front support for the mounted gun that is further supported by the short front leg. When the tripod is emplaced on flat terrain with all extensions closed, the adjustable front leg should form an angle of about 60 degrees with the ground. This places the gun on a low mount about 12 inches above the ground. To raise the tripod farther off the ground, extend the telescopic front and trail legs enough to keep the tripod level and maintain the stability of the mount.

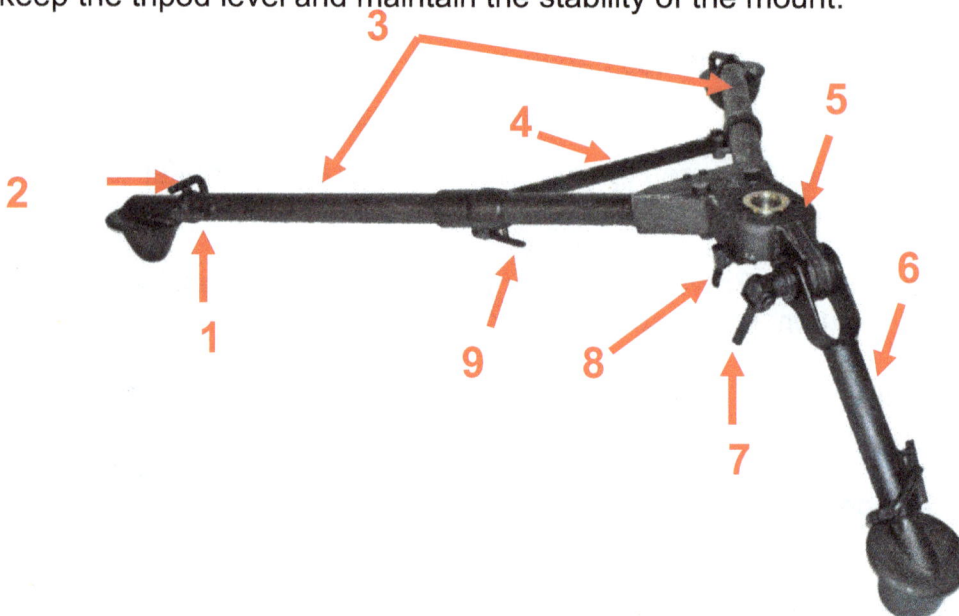

Figure 1-7 M3 tripod mount

1 – Indexing Lever Assembly	**6 – Front Leg**
2 – Leg Clamping Handle	**7 – Front Leg Clamp Handle**
3 – Trail Legs	**8 – Pintle Lock Release Cam**
4 – Traversing Bar	**9 – Rear Right Leg Sliding Sleeve**
5 – Tripod Head	

B. **Anti-aircraft Mount, M63.** The anti-aircraft mount (Figure 1-8) is a four-legged, low-silhouette portable mount used for anti-aircraft fire.

M63 Mount Shown

Figure 1-8 Antiaircraft mount, M63

The anti-aircraft firing position uses a standing position (Figure 1-9) when firing from the M63 mount. To assume the position, the gunner stands with his feet spread comfortably apart with his shoulders squarely behind the gun. When the gunner is engaging aerial targets, he grasps the upper extension handles with both hands. When engaging low-level aircraft or ground targets, he grasps the lower extension handles with both hands.

The kneeling position may be used; it has the advantage of presenting a lower profile of the gunner and also aligns the gunner's eye closer to the axis of the barrel.

Figure 1-9 Standing firing position with M63 mount

Accessories for Ground Mounts

The following paragraph explains the functions of the traversing and elevating mechanism and pintle used in the mounting of the machine gun when used in the ground configuration.

A. **Traversing and Elevating Mechanism.** The T&E mechanism (Figure 1-10) is used to engage pre-selected target areas at night or during limited visibility conditions. Record direction and elevation readings from the traversing bar and T&E mechanism. Record all readings in mils.

(1) The traversing mechanism consists of a traversing bar, slide, and screw assembly.

(a) The traversing bar, graduated in 5-roil increments, fits between the trail legs of the tripod. The traversing slide and screw assembly are clamped in place on the traversing bar by the traversing slide lock lever. When the traversing slide is locked to the traversing bar, the traversing handwheel should be centered. The traversing slide is properly mounted when the lock lever is to the rear and the traversing handwheel is positioned to the left.

(b) To make changes in direction, loosen the traversing slide lock lever and move the slide along the traversing bar. This action permits traverse of 400 mils left or right of the zero index in the center of the traversing bar. Readings on the traversing bar are taken from the left side of the traversing slide. For changes of 50 mils or less in deflection, turn the traversing handwheel of the screw assembly. This allows a traverse of 50 mils left or right of center. One click in the traversing handwheel signifies 1 mil change in direction.

(2) The elevating mechanism consists of an upper and lower elevating screw.

(a) It is connected to the gun by inserting the quick-release pin assembly through the holes in the upper elevating screw yoke and the rear mounting lugs of the receiver. A scale, graduated in mils, is fitted to the upper screw to indicate elevation. This scale is marked to show 250 mils in depression and 100 mils in elevation from the zero setting.

(b) The elevating handwheel is graduated in I-mil increments up to 50 mils and is fastened to the elevating screw by a screw lock. This setup synchronizes the handwheel graduations with those on the upper elevating screw. A spring-actuated index device produces a clicking sound when the handwheel is turned. Each click equals 1 mil change in elevation. The handwheel is turned clockwise to depress the barrel and counterclockwise to elevate.

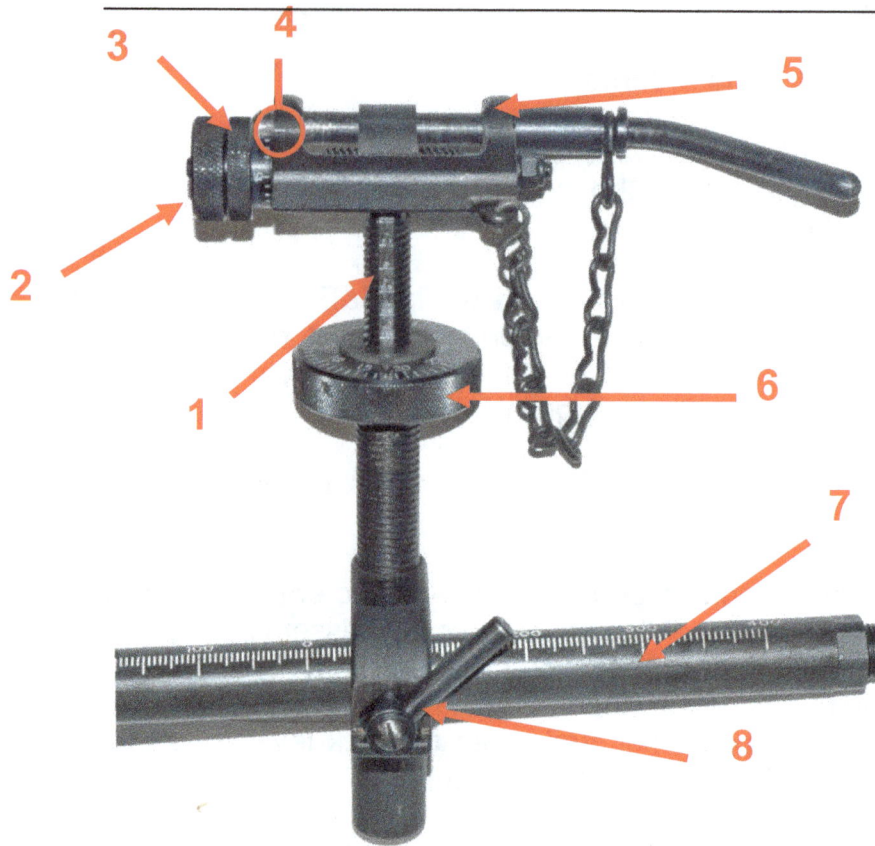

Figure 1-10 Traversing and elevating mechanism

1 – Elevation Screw Scale Plate	5 – Yoke
2 – Traversing Handwheel	6 – Elevation Handwheel
3 – Locking Nut	7 – Traversing Bar
4 – Scale	8 – Traversing Bar Lock

B. **Pintle.** The gun is connected to the tripod mount, M3, by a pintle (Figure 1-11). This pintle is semi-permanently attached to the machine gun by a pintle bolt through the front mounting hole in the receiver. The tapered stem of the pintle seats in the tripod head. It is secured by a pintle lock and spring. To release the pintle, raise the pintle lock, releasing the cam. The weight of the pintle and traversing and elevating mechanism are considered as part of the total weight of the tripod mount, M3 (44 pounds).

Figure 1-11 Pintle

Vehicular Mounts

The four principal vehicular mounts used with the caliber .50 machine gun are the truck mount, M36; the pedestal truck mount, M31C and M24A2; the commander's cupola, Ml13 armored personnel carrier; and the MK64 gun cradle.

A. **Truck Mount, M36.** This mount (Figure 1-12) consists of a cradle with a roller carriage on a circular track. The cradle can be rotated in the pintle sleeve of the carriage and can be adjusted for elevation. The carriage is guided on the track by rollers. The track is secured to the vehicle by supports.

(1) To move the gun in elevation on the M36 mount, remove the cradle locking pin and place it in the carriage handle; grasp the spade grips and elevate or depress as desired. The gun is also moved in traverse by pressure on the spade grips.

(2) To move the gun on the track, raise the brake handle lever until it is retained by the brake detent plungers. The cradle may then be moved on the track by applying pressure on the carriage handle.

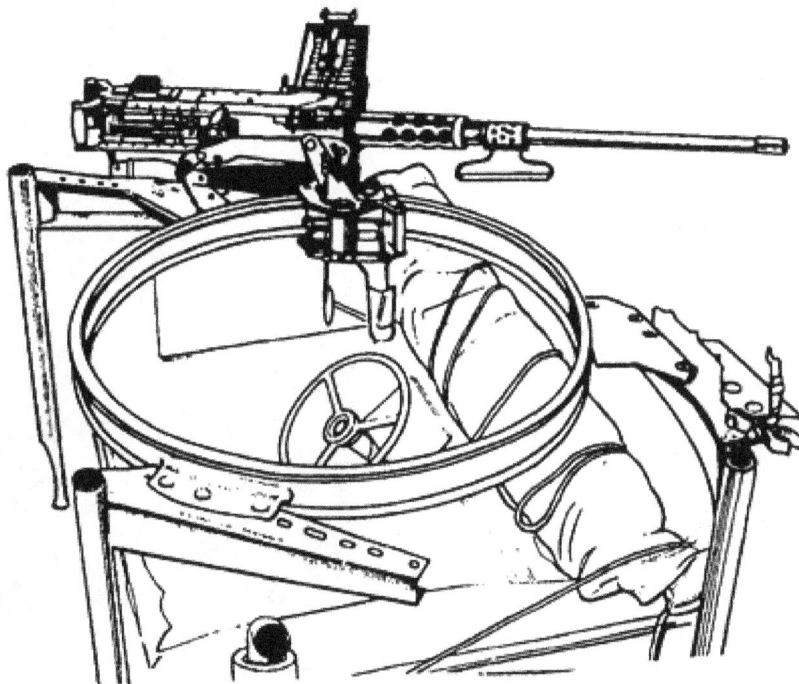

Figure 1-12 Truck mount, M36

The **vehicular firing position** (Figure 1-13) for the M2 is standing. It is assumed by constructing a solid platform to stand on, using sandbags or ammunition boxes, or, in the case of the M113 APC, using the commander's seat. The gunner must then ensure that his platform is high enough to place the spade grips of the gun about chest high. He grasps the spade grips with both hands and places both thumbs in a position to press the trigger. The gunner holds the gun tightly to his chest for stabilization; his elbows should be locked tightly to his sides. He sights over the weapon and adjusts his position by flexing his knees and leaning forward to absorb any recoil.

Figure 1-13

B. **Pedestal Truck Mount, M31C.** Pedestal mounts are component assemblies designed for installation on the 1/4-ton vehicles to support a machine gun mount. They are composed of a pintle socket, pintle clamping screw column, and braces (Figure 1-14).

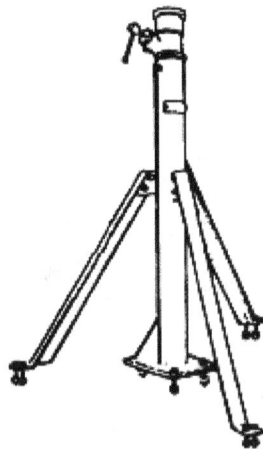

Figure 1-14 Pedestal truck mount, M31C

C. **Armored Vehicle Cupola Mount.** A caliber .50 machine gun and mount are installed in the gun support on the commander's cupola of an M113 armored personnel carrier. The machine gun can be traversed 360 degrees, elevated 53 degrees, and depressed 21 degrees maximum (Figure 1-15).

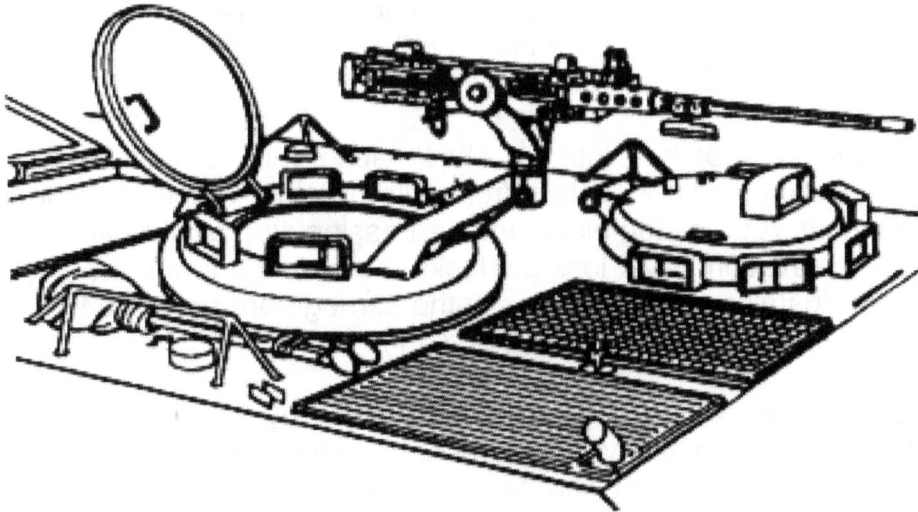

Figure 1-15 Cupola mount

D. **MK64 Gun Cradle Mount.** This vehicle mount was primarily designed for the M2. However, because of its versatility, the MK64 will also accept the MK19 (using the M2 mounting adapter assembly). The MK64 can be mounted on the following vehicles – M151 series, M966 HMMWV armament carrier, and the M113 series (Figure 1-16).

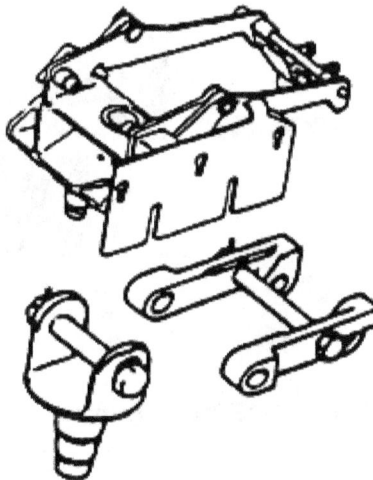

Figure 1-16 MK64 gun cradle

E. **MK93 Heavy Machine Gun Mounting System.** This MK93 machine gun mount is a new (2004) stronger design by the U.S. Army (Figure 1-17). The mount accepts the M2HB 12.7mm machine gun or the MK19 40mm machine gun and is designed for use on HMMWVs, trucks, and armored vehicles. With its small pintle, it fits into a variety of tripods, pedestals, and the Universal Pintle Adapter (UPA). The left rail supports an interface plate that accepts a variety of quick-removable ammo can holders. The M2HB weapon is held in place by front and rear stainless-steel ball lock pins. A slider system with two hydraulic shock absorbers reduces firing shock in both recoil and counter recoil for the M2HB. The normal recoil of 1200 pounds is reduced to less than 500 pounds peak.

The MK19 weapon that has internal shock absorbers is held in place with a stainless-steel rear pin and 2 studs in front, allowing the weapon to slide back and forth in the mount. A train stop block and depression stop assembly provide travel stop limits. An elevation travel lock pin locks the carriage to the cradle, making it much easier to install a weapon. Holes in the carriage are provided for installation of armor brackets and Armor Shield (M35-021).

An optional Adapter Kit (M35-800) manufactured by Military Systems Group, provides for installation of the M240 or the M249 weapons. It is not recommended to use this machine gun mount with the swing arm system or in naval applications due to its fabrication using carbon steel.

Characteristics:
Height - 6.8 inches
Width - 10.0 inches
Length - 22.0 inches
Weight - 30.2 pounds

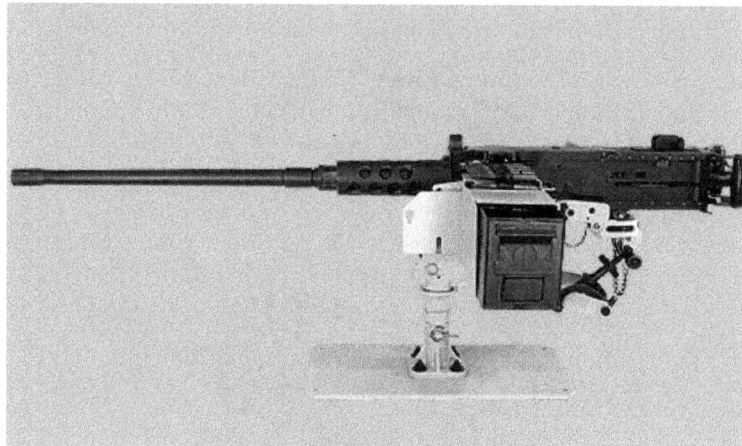

Figure 1-17 MK93 gun cradle

Section 2

Maintenance

Safety Rules- The following safety rules apply at all times to all weapons.

1. Treat every weapon as if it were loaded.
2. Never point a weapon at anything you do not intend to shoot.
3. Keep your finger straight and off the trigger until you are ready to fire.
4. Keep the weapon on SAFE until you are ready to fire.

Weapons Conditions

A. <u>Condition 1</u>: Bolt forward, round in the chamber, ammunition in the feed way, cover closed (full load- the weapon has been charged twice).

B. <u>Condition 2</u>: Bolt forward, rounds on the feed way, 1st round against the cartridge stop, no ammunition in the chamber, cover closed (half load- the weapon has been charged once).

C. <u>Condition 3</u>: Bolt forward, 1st round engaged by the belt holding pawl, no ammunition in the chamber, cover closed.

D. <u>Condition 4</u>: Bolt forward, no ammunition on the feed way, no ammunition in the chamber, cover closed.

Safety

The paramount consideration while training with the machine gun is safety. It is imperative that the weapon be cleared properly before disassembly and inspection.

Clearing the M2 BMG in Condition 1

A. Unlock the bolt-latch release (Single-shot mode) (Figure 2-1).

Figure 2-1 Single-shot mode

B. Pull the retracting slide handle to the rear and hold it to the rear (to prevent slamfire from the bolt not being locked fully to the rear) (Figure 2-2).

Figure 2-2 Pulling and holding slide handle to the rear

C. Raise the cover (Figure 2-3).

Figure 2-3 Raising the feedway cover

D. Remove the ammunition belt from the feedway (Figure 2-4).

Figure 2-4 Removing the ammunition belt

E. Visually and physically inspect the chamber and the T-slot to ensure that they hold no rounds (Figures 2-5a & b).

Figure 2-5a Clear chamber

Figure 2-5b Clear T-slot

1) If there is a round on the T-slot, pull the bolt an additional 1/16" to the rear (Figure 2-6).

2) Push the round up and out of the T-slot by reaching under the gun to force the round up the face of the bolt.

Figure 2-6 Round in T-slot

F. Put the retracting slide handle forward, and then push the bolt latch release to send the bolt forward.

G. The gun is now clear.

Clearing the M2 BMG in Condition 4

A. Unlock the bolt-latch release and raise the cover (Figure 2-7).

Figure 2-7 Raising the feedway cover

B. Pull the bolt to the rear. Examine the chamber and the T-slot to ensure that they hold no rounds (Figure 2-8).

Figure 2-8 Retracting the bolt to observe the chamber and T-slot

C. The gun is now clear.

Disassembling the .50 BMG

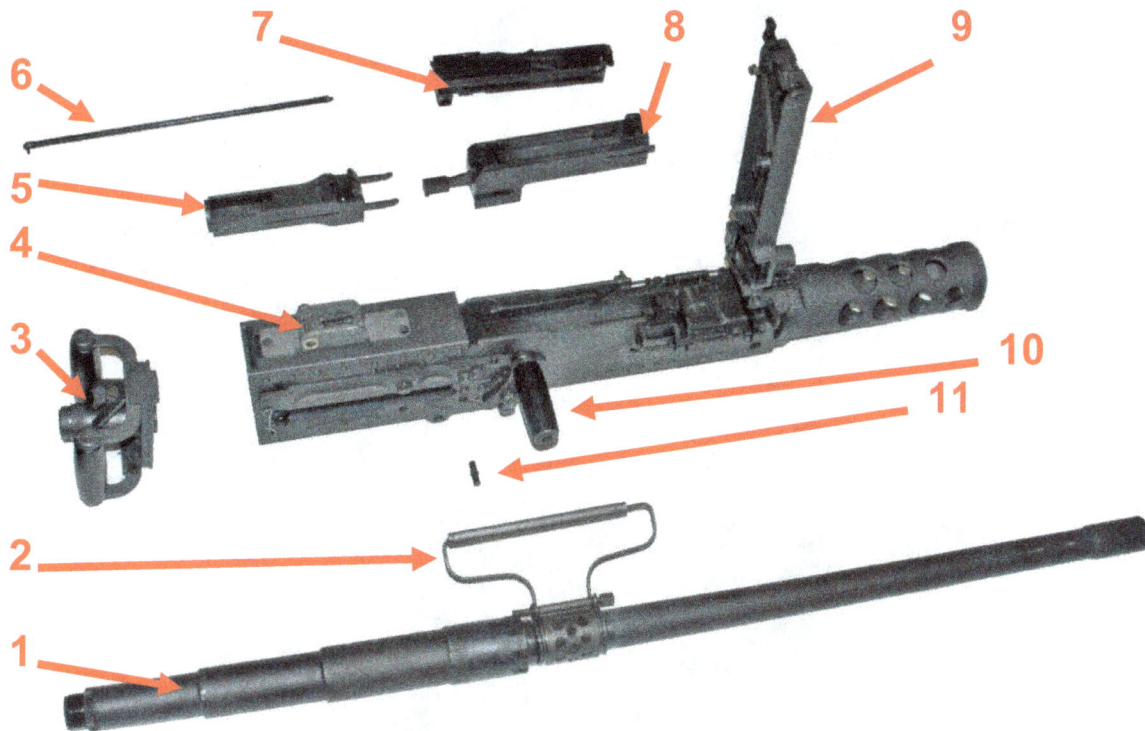

Figure 2-9 M2 .50 BMG components

1 – Barrel
2 – Barrel Carrying Handle
3 – Backplate
4 – Receiver
5 – Buffer Assembly
6 – Driving Spring Assembly

7 – Bolt
8 – Barrel Extension
9 – Feedway Cover
10 – Retracting Handle
11 – Bolt Stud

NOTE: Place the weapon's parts on a flat, clean surface with the muzzle oriented in a safe direction. Wooden blocks or use of the tripod facilitate the handling of the BMG.

When the operator begins to disassemble the weapon, it should be done in the following order:

A. **Barrel Group.**

- Open feed tray cover (Figure 2-10)

Figure 2-10 Raising the feedway cover

- Retract recoiling parts group with retracting handle approximately 3/8". Observe the alignment of the barrel-locking spring lug in the 3/8-inch hole in the right side plate of the receiver (just below the feed way exit) (Figure 2-11).

Figure 2-11 Retracting the bolt approximately 3/8"

- Place the smallest loop of a caliber .50 link, or suitable spacer, between the trunnion block and the barrel extension (Figure 2-12).

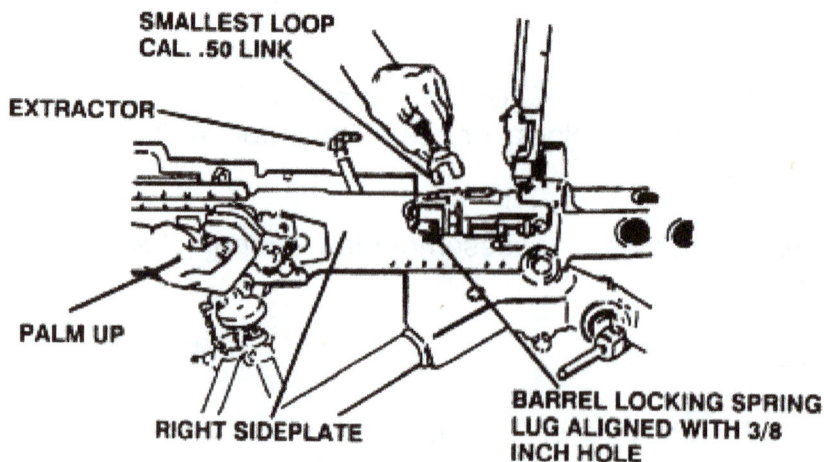

Figure 2-12 Aligning the lug on the barrel-locking spring with the 3/8-inch hole in the right side plate

---

- Unscrew the barrel (to the left) from the receiver (Figure 2-13). Be careful not to damage the threads or barrel locking notches when setting the barrel down. Pull back slightly on the retracting slide handle and remove the link or spacer from the receiver.

Figure 2-13 Removing the barrel

B. **Backplate Group.** Ensure that the bolt latch release is up, free of the bolt latch release lock. If it is not, push down on the bolt latch release and turn the buffer tube sleeve to the right to free it (Figure 2-14). The bolt must be forward before the backplate is removed. If the bolt is to the rear, push down on the bolt latch release, place palm up on the retracting slide handle, and ease the bolt forward. The backplate latch lock and latch are below the buffer tube. Pull out on the lock and up on the latch; remove the backplate by lifting it straight up (Figure 2-15).

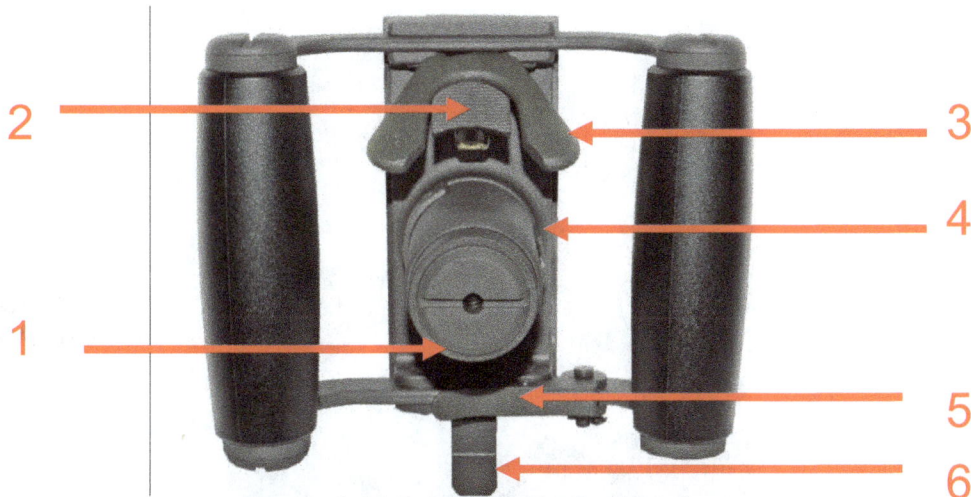

Figure 2-14 Releasing the bolt latch

1- Buffer Tube Sleeve
2- Bolt Latch Release
3- Trigger

4- Bolt Latch Release Lock
5- Backplate Lock
6- Backplate Latch

CAUTION

Care must be taken to prevent the bolt from slamming forward with the barrel removed.

Figure 2-15 Removing the backplate

C. **Driving Spring Rod Assembly.** The inner and outer driving springs and driving spring rod are located inside the receiver next to the right side plate (Figure 2-16). Push in on the head of the driving spring rod and push to the left to remove the driving spring rod retaining pin from its seat in the right side plate. Pull the driving spring assembly to the rear and out of the receiver.

WARNING
Never attempt to cock the gun while the backplate is off and the driving spring assembly is in place. If the backplate is off and the driving spring assembly is compressed, the retaining pin on the driving spring rod can slip from its seat in the side plate and could cause serious injury to anyone behind the gun.

Bolt Latch

Driving Spring Rod Assembly

Figure 2-16 Removing the driving spring rod assembly

D. **Bolt Stud.** Grasp the retracting slide handle and give it a quick jerk, freeing the bolt from the barrel extension. Align the collar of the bolt stud with the clearance hole in the bolt slot on the right side plate, and remove the bolt stud (Figure 2-17). If the bolt is accidentally moved all the way to the rear, the bolt latch will engage in the bolt latch notches in the top of the bolt. If this occurs, raise the bolt latch (left of the trigger lever) and push the bolt forward to align the bolt stud with the clearance hole (Figure 2-18).

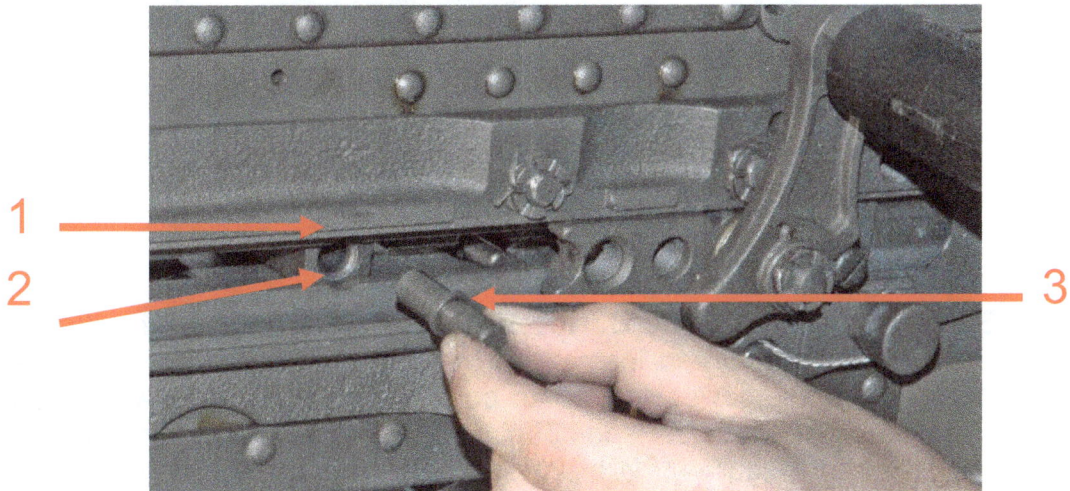

Figure 2-17 Removing the bolt stud

1 – Shoulder   2 – Bolt Stud   3 – Clearance Hole

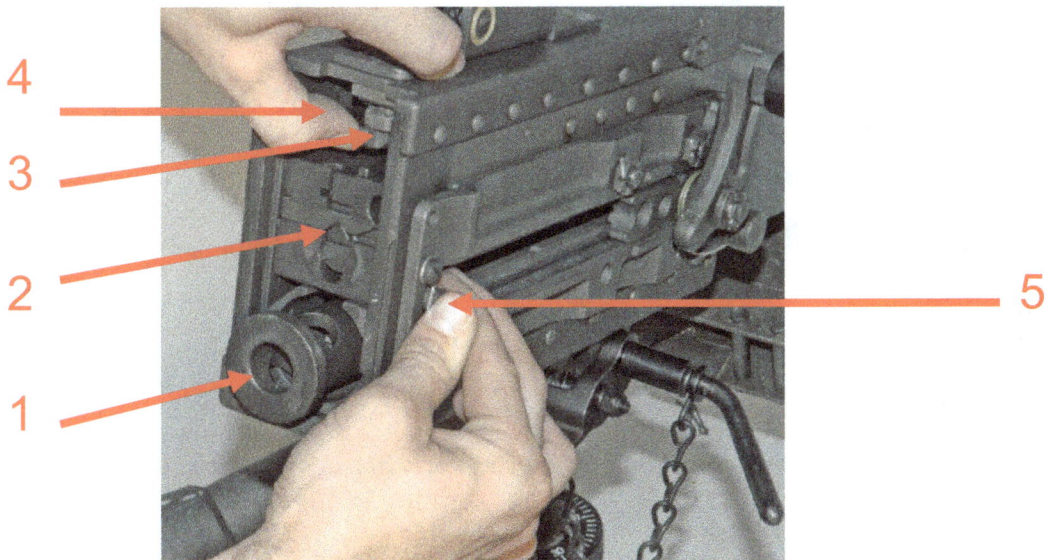

Figure 2-18 Removing the bolt

1 – **Buffer Assembly**   4 – **Trigger Lever**
2 – **Bolt**   5 – **Bolt Stud**
3 – **Bolt Latch**

E. **Bolt Group.** After freeing the bolt, slide it to the rear and out of the receiver (Figure 2-19). Place the bolt down on its right side (with the extractor arm up) so that the extractor will not fall from the bolt.

Figure 2-19 Removing the bolt from the receiver

F. **Barrel Buffer Body Group and Barrel Extension Group.** Insert the drift of a combination tool or other pointed instrument through the hole in the lower rear corner of the right side plate. Push in on the barrel buffer body lock. At the same time, place one hand in the receiver and push the barrel extension group and barrel buffer group to the rear (Figures 2-20a & 2-20b). Remove the barrel buffer group and barrel extension group from the receiver. Separate the two groups by pushing forward on the tips of the accelerator (Figure 2-21).

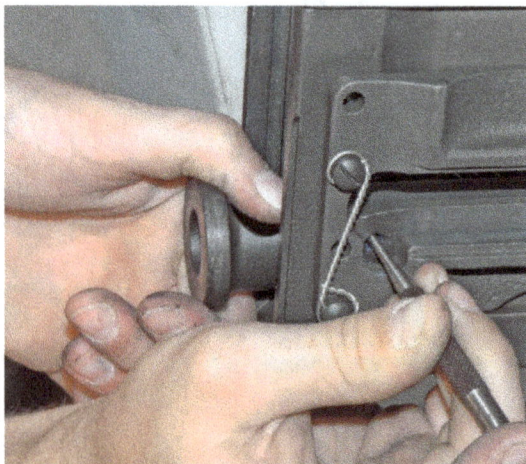

Figure 2-20a

Figure 2-20b

Removing barrel buffer group and barrel extension group

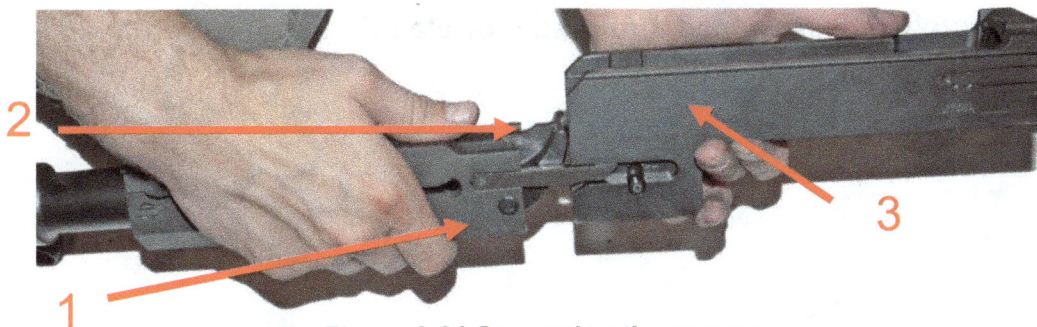

Figure 2-21 Separating the groups

1 – Barrel Buffer Body Group
2 – Accelerator Tips

3 – Barrel Extension Group

G. **Barrel Buffer Assembly.** Pull the barrel buffer assembly from the rear of the barrel buffer body group. The barrel buffer assembly will not be disassembled (Figure 2-22). This completes general disassembly.

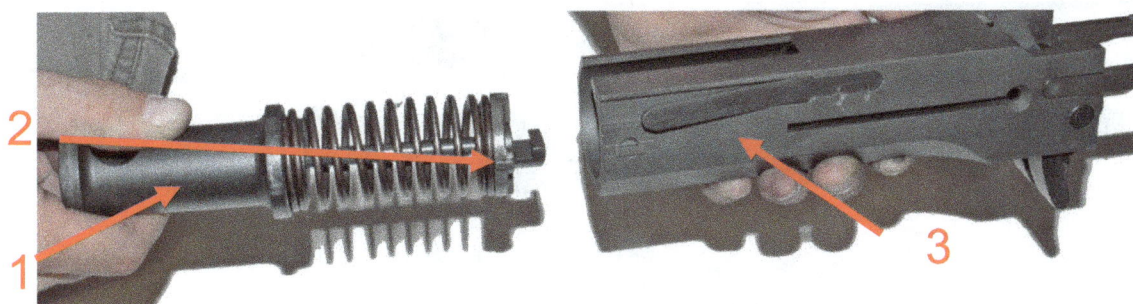

Figure 2-22 Separating the barrel buffer assembly from the barrel buffer body group

1 – Cross Groove in the Piston Rod
2 – Buffer Assembly

3 – Barrel Buffer Body Group

M2 completely disassembled and ready for cleaning and inspection

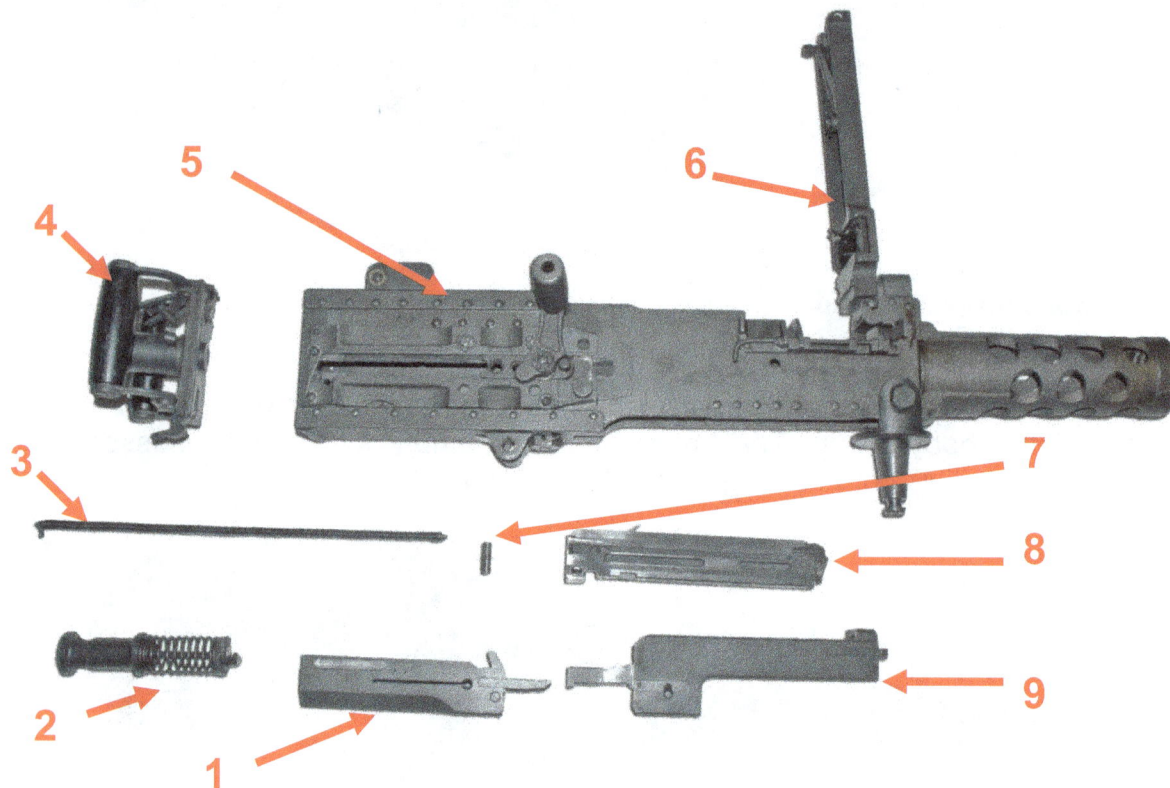

Figure 2-23 Disassembled M2

1 – Barrel Buffer Body Group
2 – Buffer Assembly
3 – Backplate
4 – Receiver
5 – Receiver

6 – Feedway Cover
7 – Bolt Stud
8 – Barrel Extension
9 – Barrel Extension

Cleaning, Lubrication and Preventive Maintenance for the M2 BMG

To ensure proper care of the MG, it is necessary to have a system of maintenance or an SOP for the frequency of cleaning. Each gun should be cleaned as soon after firing as possible and each time it is exposed to field conditions. Under combat conditions, the gun should be cleaned and oiled daily. Under extreme climatic and combat conditions, it maybe necessary to clean and lubricate more frequently. Under ideal conditions, where the gun is not used and is stored in a clean, dry place, it may only be necessary to inspect, clean, and lubricate every 5 days. The gun should be disassembled, cleaned, and oiled in a clean, dry location. If possible, keep the gun covered with a gun cover, canvas, tarpaulin, or poncho when not in use.

A. **Routine Care and Cleaning.** Before firing (when the situation permits), take the following steps to ensure efficient functioning of the machine gun:
• Disassemble the gun into its major groups or assemblies.
• Clean the bore and chamber, and lightly oil them.
• Clean all metal parts thoroughly with CLP. See paragraph 2-3f for lubrication procedures.

B. **Care and Cleaning Under Unusual Conditions.** Extreme cold, hot, dry, and tropical climates affect the gun and its functioning. Care should be taken under these climatic conditions to ensure that the gun is cleaned daily with the prescribed lubricants and protected from the elements by some sort of cover if possible. Further information on care and cleaning of the gun under unusual climatic conditions can be found in TM 9-1005-213-10.

C. **Care and Cleaning of M3 Mount and Accessories.** The mount and accessories, such as the ammunition chest and spare parts, should also be kept clean and lubricated. Painted surfaces should be spot painted when necessary. Moving surfaces should be inspected and oiled with the prescribed lubricant. All external surfaces of the mount should be kept clean and lightly oiled. Be particularly careful that the pintle bushing is clean and lightly oiled, and that the pintle lock release cam is well-lubricated and free from grit. The sleeve lock indexing levers and telescopic legs should be clean and lubricated enough for ease in use. The mount should be cleaned and oiled with the same regularity and in the same manner as the gun.

D. **Maintenance and Inspection.** Units must establish guidelines and conduct regular maintenance and inspection to keep the machine gun and its mounts in operational conditions.

(1) *Gun maintenance.* The importance of a thorough knowledge of care, cleaning, and maintenance of the machine gun cannot be overemphasized because these actions determine whether or not the gun will function properly when needed. The bore and chamber must be properly maintained to preserve accuracy. Because of

the close fit of working surfaces and the high speed at which the gun operates, the receiver and moving parts must be kept clean, correctly lubricated, and free from burrs, rust, dirt, or grease to ensure proper, efficient functioning.

(2) *Mount maintenance.* The care, cleaning, lubrication, and adjustment of the mounts used with the gun are no less important. The functioning of the gun and mount together determine overall effectiveness. All accessories and equipment used with the gun and mount, including ammunition, must also be properly maintained.

(3) *Inspection.* When inspected, the machine gun should be completely disassembled. Inspecting personnel should look for dirt, cracks, burrs, and rust.

E. **Inspection Checklist.** Table 2-1 is an inspection checklist to be used as a guide for crewmembers or inspecting personnel to ensure that the gun and equipment are properly maintained.

UNIT	INSPECTION
1. GUN	
a. Barrel	Inspect the bore and chamber for rust. See that they are clean and lightly oiled.
b. Moving Parts	See that they are clean and lightly oiled. Operate the retracting slide handle and bolt latch release several times to see that the parts function without excessive friction.
c. Headspace and Timing	Check with the gauges to ensure that headspace and timing are correct.
d. Rear Sight and Windage Knob	Ensure that the sight is in good condition, clean, free of grease or dirt, and lightly oiled. Elevation should be set at 1,000, windage zero, and the sight should be down.
2. MOUNT	See that it is clean, lightly lubricated, and that all clamps are securely tightened. It should function properly and be complete.
3. SPARE PARTS AND TOOLS	Inspect to see that they are clean and lightly oiled. See that spare parts kits are complete and in good condition. Replacement parts should be requisitioned and newly drawn parts examined.
4. T & E	See that it is clean, lightly lubricated, and that both hand wheels work properly.

| 5. AMMUNITION | See that ammunition is properly stored, and that boxes and ammunition are in good condition and not oiled. |

F. **Lubrications.** Use cleaner, lubricant, preservative to clean the machine gun. As its name implies, it cleans, lubricates, and preserves all in one application.

(1) After cleaning the gun with CLP, wipe it dry and reapply a thin coating. Allow this thin coat to dry on the parts for a short time before reassembly. CLP deposits a thin coating on the metal which minimizes carbon buildup and prevents foreign material from sticking. It is this coating that provides the frictionless operation of the weapon parts, not liquid oil deposited on them. A gun treated with CLP will operate better and remain clean longer than one treated with any other cleaning material. Use of CLP will reduce maintenance costs and extend the life of the weapon.

(2) Rifle bore cleaner is a cleaning solvent which can be used to clean powder residue, carbon, and dirt from weapons. RBC does not preserve or lubricate a weapon. If you clean a weapon with RBC, dry the weapon and lubricate it with lubricating oil, semi fluid (LSA); lubricating oil, special purpose (PL-S); or lubricating oil, general purpose (PL-M). The use of these oils will cause sand or grit to stick to the weapon. RBC and oil should be used only when CLP is not available.

Maintenance Procedures

There are certain actions that must be taken before, during, and after firing to maintain the gun properly. See Table 2-2 for a pre-operation checklist.

PART	BEFORE	DURING FIRING	AFTER
Bore	Make sure it is clear and clean		Clean and oil
Moving Parts	Oil lightly and test for worn or broken parts.	Lubricate working parts. Observe the function of the gun.	Inspect, clean, and oil lightly.
Headspace and Timing	Check adjustment by gauge and correct if necessary.	Watched for bulged cases to prevent a ruptured case. If a separated case occurs, remove it and readjust headspace.	Check adjustment.
Rear Sight and Windage Knob	See that the sight is clean and functions properly. Set to 1,000, and windage to zero.	Keep properly set.	Clean and oil; set at 1,000 and windage to zero.
Spare Parts and Tools	Clean and oil spare parts and tools. Check kits for completeness.	Keep available.	Clean and oil. Check and replace damaged or missing parts.
Ammunition	Have an adequate Supply, clean, correctly loaded, and in good condition.	Keep correctly aligned with the feedway; check resupply. Protect from sun, moisture, and dirt. Watch for link stoppage.	Clean, store carefully, and replenish supply.

Maintenance Under NBC Conditions

If contamination is anticipated, apply oil to all outer metal surfaces of the weapon. DO NOT OIL AMMUNITION. Keep the weapon covered as much as possible. If the weapon is contaminated, decontaminate it as prescribed by FM 3-5 and then clean and lubricate it.

Assembling the .50 BMG

To assemble the gun, replace the groups and assemblies in reverse order of their removal in disassembly.

A. **Barrel Buffer Assembly and Barrel Buffer Body Group.** Replace the barrel buffer assembly in the barrel buffer body group, with the key on the spring guide to the right. This key must fit in its slot in the right side of the barrel buffer body. Turn the barrel buffer tube until the screwdriver slot (in the rear of the tube) is vertical and the arrow is pointing to the right. The stud on the tube lock will now engage the serrations in the barrel buffer tube to keep the tube from turning. Push the barrel buffer assembly fully forward (Figure 2-24).

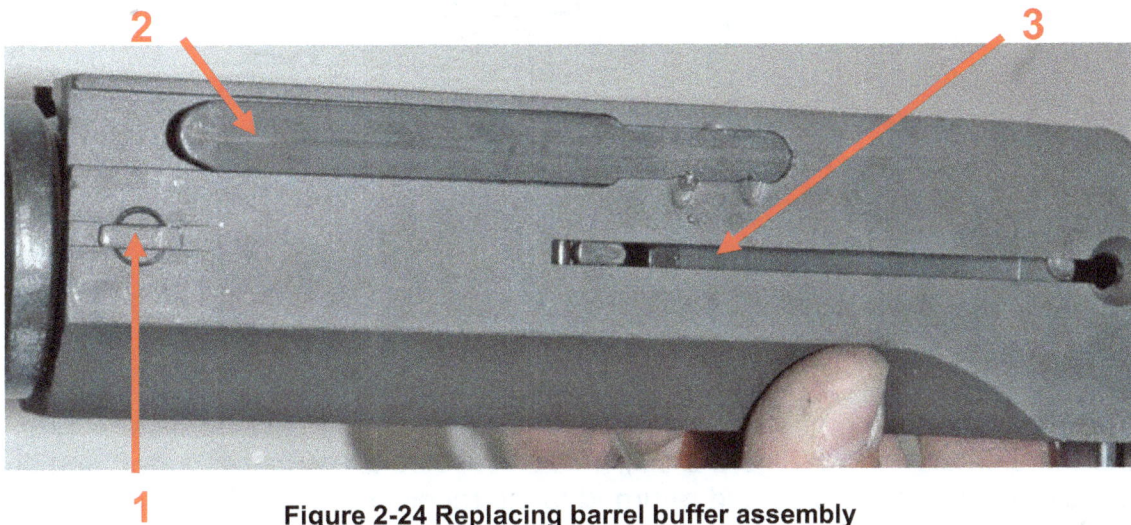

Figure 2-24 Replacing barrel buffer assembly

1 – Barrel Buffer Guide   3 – Barrel Buffer Spring Guide Key
2 – Barrel Buffer Body Spring Lock

B. **Barrel Buffer Group and Barrel Extension Group.** To join the two groups together, hold the barrel buffer group in the right hand, with the index finger supporting the accelerator. Join the notch on the shank of the barrel extension group with the cross-groove in the pistol rod of the barrel buffer assembly. At the same time, align the breech lock depressors with their guide ways in the sides of the barrel extension, ensuring that the tips of the accelerator are against the rear end of the barrel extension (claws against the shank) (Figures 2-25a & 2-25b). Push the groups together. As the accelerator rotates to the rear, press down on its tips to ensure positive locking of groups. Place the groups in the receiver, and push them forward until the barrel buffer body spring lock snaps into position. When the parts are properly locked in place, the barrel buffer tube should protrude about 1 1/8 inches from the rear of the barrel buffer body group.

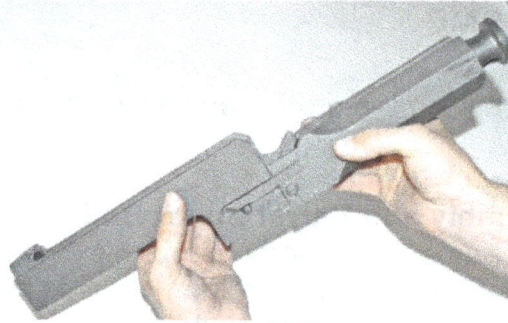

Figure 2-25a

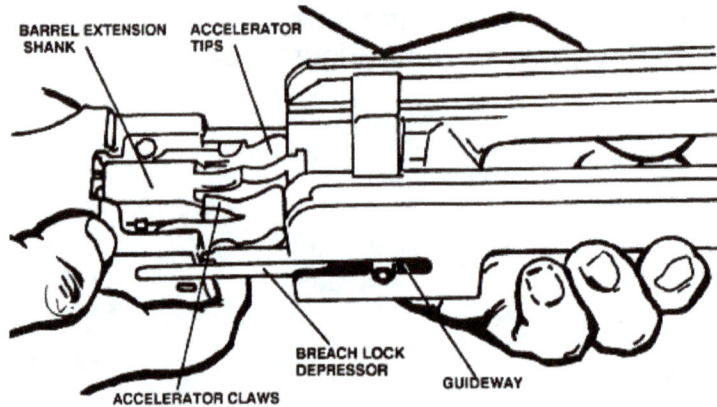

Figure 2-25b
Joining the barrel extension and barrel buffer group

C. **Bolt.** Place the bolt in the receiver, with the top of the cocking lever **forward** and the extractor down (Figure 2-26). The barrel extension, barrel buffer, and bolt groups may be assembled and returned to the receiver together (Figure 2-27).

Figure 2-26 Placing the bolt onto the barrel extension and barrel buffer group

Figure 2-27 Returning the barrel extension, barrel buffer, and bolt groups together

CAUTION - Before inserting the bolt group, ensure bolt switch mechanism is positioned on **L** (left-hand) feed for the weapon.

Once the assembly is inserted into the receiver as far as possible, press upwards on the bolt latch, which will allow the assembly to seat forward fully on the barrel extension (Figure 2-28).

Figure 2-28 Pressing up on the bolt latch to seat the assembly fully

D. **Bolt Stud.** Align the stud hole in the bolt with the clearance hole and replace the bolt stud, ensuring that the collar of the stud is inside the side plate (Figure 2-29).

Figure 2-29 Replacing the bolt stud

E. **Drive Spring Assembly.** Press up on the bolt latch, and push the bolt all the way forward by pushing on the bolt stud only. Place the end of the drive spring rod in its hole in the rear of the bolt, and push forward on the drive spring assembly and the barrel buffer tube. Press in and to the right on the head of the drive spring rod and place the retaining pin in its seat in the right side plate (Figures 2-30a & 2-30b).

Figure 2-30a   **Figure 2-30b**
Inserting drive spring and drive spring rod assembly

NOTE: At this time, the barrel buffer tube should be completely inside the receiver. If not, the barrel buffer body spring is not properly seated.

F. **Backplate Group.** Hold the backplate with the latch down and the trigger up; place the backplate guides in their guide ways. Hold out on the latch lock and tap the backplate into position until the latch snaps into place (Figure 2-31). Release the latch lock and pull up on the backplate group to ensure it is firmly seated.

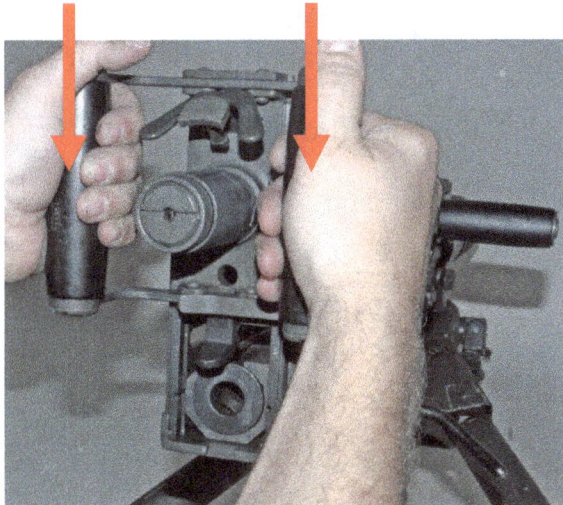

Figure 2-31 Replacing the backplate group

CAUTION
Do not use the driving rod to drive the bolt forward from the rear position. This may damage the drive spring group and cause a stoppage.

G. **Barrel.** Pull the retracting slide handle to the rear until the lug on the barrel locking spring is visible through the 3/8-inch hole in the right side plate. Place the smallest loop of a caliber .50 link, or suitable spacer, between the trunnion block and the barrel extension. Screw the barrel all the way into the barrel extension; then unscrew the barrel two notches. Remove the link and close the cover. This completes general assembly.

Function Check Procedures

A function check must be performed as soon as the weapon is assembled to ensure that the weapon has been assembled correctly. The following procedures should be taken to check the function of the weapon.

A. Place the weapon in the single-shot mode.

B. Open the cover and lock the bolt to the rear (bolt should stay to rear while in the single-shot mode).

C. Hold the retractor handles, press the bolt latch release, and ride the bolt forward.

D. Press down on the trigger; weapon should fire. (Check T-slot to ensure that the firing pin does protrude.)

E. Place the weapon in the automatic-fire mode.

F. Pull the retractor slide handle to the rear and hold. (Bolt should not lock to rear.)

G. Release the pressure on the slide handles and ride the bolt forward.

H. Make sure the firing pin does not protrude.

I. Press the trigger; weapon should fire.

J. Make sure the firing pin does protrude.

NOTE- Before firing a newly assembled weapon, first set the headspace and timing. Chapter 3 describes these procedures.

Section 3

Operation and Function

Safety Rules- The following safety rules apply at all times to all weapons.

5. Treat every weapon as if it were loaded.
6. Never point a weapon at anything you do not intend to shoot.
7. Keep your finger straight and off the trigger until you are ready to fire.
8. Keep the weapon on SAFE until you are ready to fire.

Weapons Conditions

A. <u>Condition 1</u>: Bolt forward, round in the chamber, ammunition in the feed way, cover closed (full load- the weapon has been charged twice).

B. <u>Condition 2</u>: Bolt forward, rounds on the feed way, 1st round against the cartridge stop, no ammunition in the chamber, cover closed (half load- the weapon has been charged once).

C. <u>Condition 3</u>: Bolt forward, 1st round engaged by the belt holding pawl, no ammunition in the chamber, cover closed.

D. <u>Condition 4</u>: Bolt forward, no ammunition on the feed way, no ammunition in the chamber, cover closed.

Safety

The paramount consideration while training with the machine gun is safety. It is imperative that the weapon be cleared properly before disassembly and inspection.

Clearing the M2 BMG in Condition 1

A. Unlock the bolt-latch release (Single-shot mode) (Figure 3-1).

Figure 3-1 Single-shot mode

B. Pull the retracting slide handle to the rear and hold it to the rear (to prevent slam fire from the bolt not being locked fully to the rear) (Figure 3-2).

Figure3-2 Pulling and holding slide handle to the rear

C. Raise the cover (Figure 3-3).

Figure 3-3 Raising the feedway cover

D. Remove the ammunition belt from the feedway (Figure 3-4).

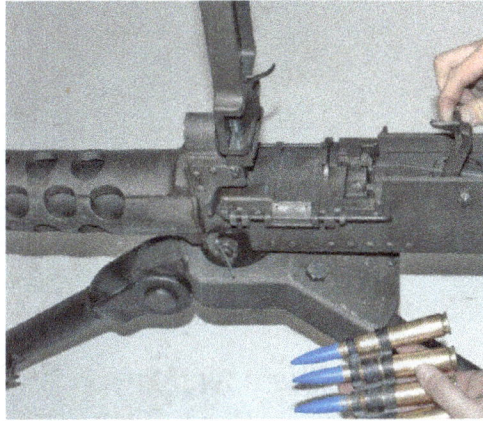

Figure 3-4 Removing the ammunition belt

E. Visually and physically inspect the chamber and the T-slot to ensure that they hold no rounds (Figures 3-5a & 3-5b).

Figure 3-5a Clear chamber

Figure3-5b Clear T-slot

1) If there is a round on the T-slot, pull the bolt an additional 1/16" to the rear (Figure 3-6).

2) Push the round up and out of the T-slot by reaching under the gun to force the round up the face of the bolt.

Figure 3-6 Round in T-slot

F. Put the retracting slide handle forward, and then push the bolt latch release to send the bolt forward.

G. The gun is now clear.

Clearing the M2 BMG in Condition 4

A. Unlock the bolt-latch release and raise the cover (Figure 3-7).

Figure 3-7 Raising the feedway cover

B. Pull the bolt to the rear. Examine the chamber and the T-slot to ensure that they hold no rounds (Figure 3-8).

Figure 3-8 Retracting the bolt to observe the chamber and T-slot

C. The gun is now clear.

Cycle of Function

The cycle of functioning is broken down into basic steps: feeding, chambering, locking, firing, unlocking, extracting, ejecting, and cocking. Some of these steps may occur at the same time.

A. **Feeding**. Feeding is the act of placing a cartridge in the receiver, approximately in back of the barrel, ready for chambering. When the bolt is fully forward and the top is closed, the ammunition belt is held in the feed way by the belt-holding pawl (Figure 3-9).

(1) As the bolt is moved to the rear, the belted ammunition is moved over and then held in a stationary position by the belt-holding pawl. At the same time, the belt-feed pawl rides up and over the link, holding the first round in place. When the bolt is all the way to the rear, the belt-feed slide moves out far enough to allow the belt-feed pawl spring to force the pawl up between the first and second rounds (Figure 3-10).

BELT-HOLDING PAWL

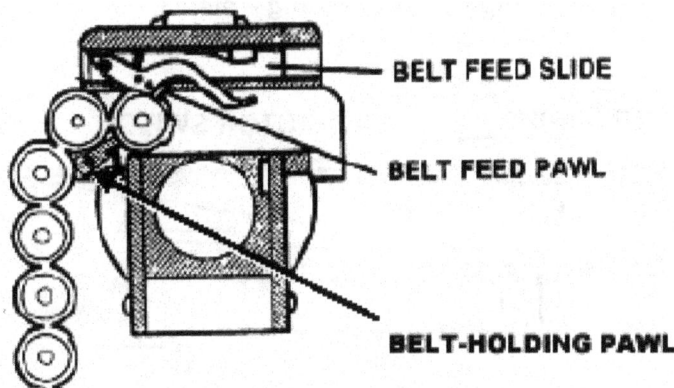

Figure 3-9 Feeding--step 1

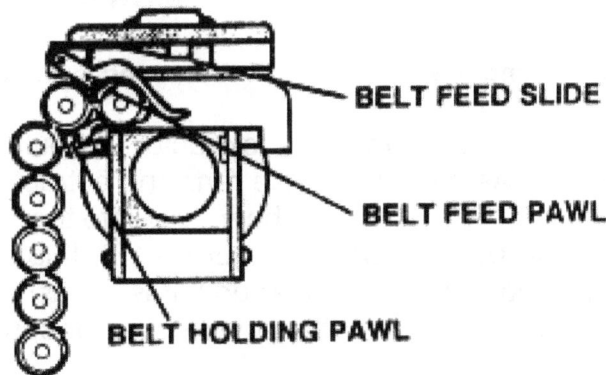

Figure 3-10 Feeding – step 2

(2) As the bolt moves forward, the belt-feed slide is moved back into the receiver, pulling with it the next linked cartridge. When the bolt reaches the fully forward position, the belt-holding pawl will snap into place behind the second linked cartridge (Figure 3-11), holding it in place. The extractor will then grasp the rim of the first cartridge, preparing to release it from the belt on the next rearward motion (Figure 3-12).

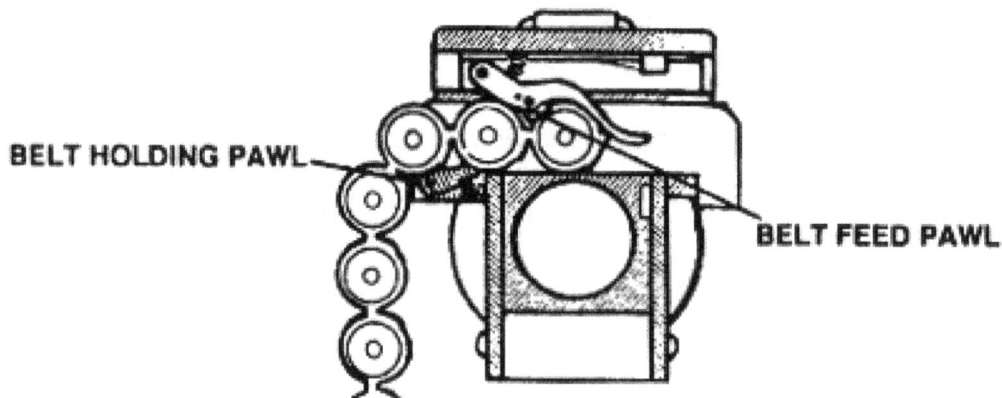

Figure 3-11 Feeding – step 3

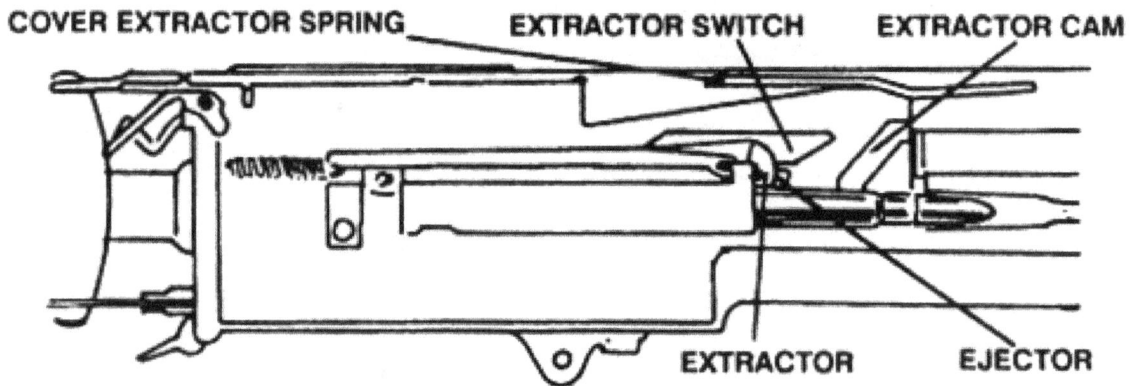

Figure 3-12 Feeding – Withdrawing the first round from the feed way

(3) As the bolt then moves to the rear, the extractor will pull the cartridge with it, releasing it from the belt. As it moves to the rear, the extractor is forced down by the extractor cam, causing the cartridge to be moved into the T-slot in the bolt face, preparing the cartridge to be chambered (Figure 3-13). It is connected under the extractor switch on the side of the receiver until it is repositioned by the forward movement of the bolt, and pressure of the cover extractor spring forces it over the next round.

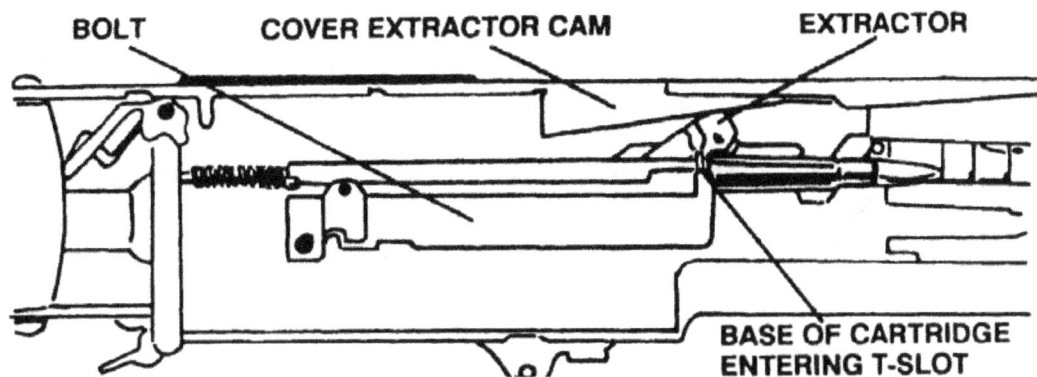

Figure 3-13 Feeding – cartridge entering the T-slot in the bolt

B. **Chambering.** Chambering is placing the cartridge into the chamber of the weapon. During this cycle, the bolt moves forward, carrying the cartridge in the T-slot in a direct route to the chamber of the weapon. At the same time, the extractor rides up the extractor cam and when the bolt is fully forward, the extractor grasps the next linked cartridge (Figure 3-14).

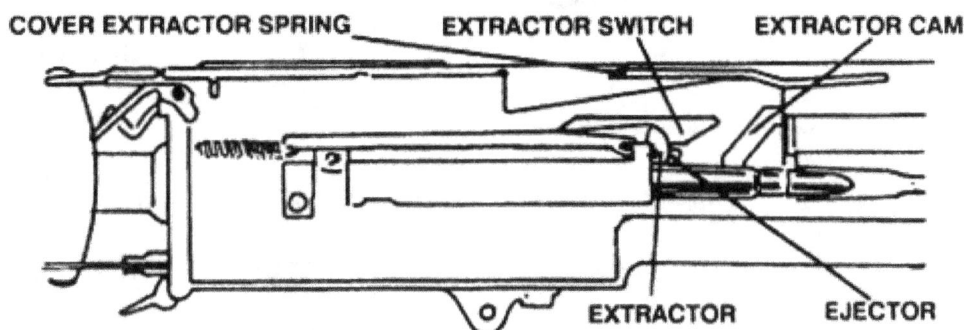

Figure 3-14 Chambering – new round aligned with the chamber

C. **Locking.** The bolt is locked to the barrel and barrel extension.

(1) Initially, the bolt is forced forward in counter-recoil by the energy stored in the driving spring assembly and the compressed buffer disks. At the start of counter-recoil, the barrel buffer body tube lock keeps the accelerator tips from bounding up too soon and catching in the breech lock recess in the bolt. After the bolt travels forward about 5 inches, the lower rear projection of the bolt strikes the tips of the accelerator, turning the accelerator forward. This action unlocks the barrel extension from the barrel buffer body group and releases the barrel buffer spring. The barrel buffer spring expands, forcing the piston rod forward.

(2) Since the cross groove in the piston rod engages the notch on the barrel extension shank, the barrel extension and barrel are also forced forward by the action of the barrel buffer spring. Some of the forward motion of the bolt is

transmitted to the barrel extension through the accelerator. As the accelerator rotates forward, the front of the accelerator speeds up the barrel extension; at the same time, the accelerator tips slow down the bolt.

(3) Locking begins 1 1/8 inches before the recoiling groups (bolt, barrel extension, and barrel) are fully forward. The breech lock in the barrel extension rides up the breech lock cam in the bottom of the receiver into the breech lock recess in the bottom of the bolt, locking the recoiling groups together. The recoiling groups are completely locked together three-fourths of an inch before the groups are fully forward (Figure 3-15).

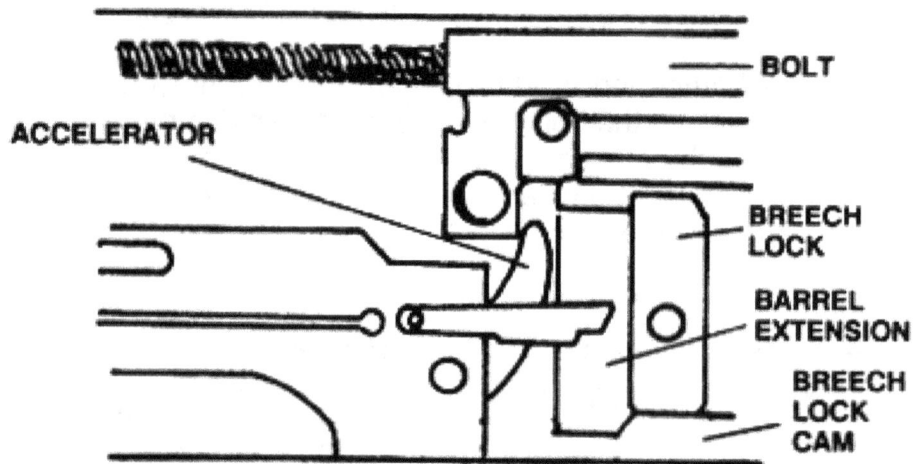

Figure 3-15 Locking – recoiling groups locked together

D. **Firing.** The firing pin is released, igniting the primer of the cartridge.

(1) As the trigger is pressed down, it pivots on the trigger pin so that the trigger cam on the inside of the backplate engages and raises the rear end of the trigger lever. This part in turn pivots on the trigger lever pin assembly, causing the front end of the trigger lever to press down on the top of the sear stud. The sear is forced down until the hooked notch of the firing pin extension is disengaged from the sear notch. The firing pin and firing pin extension are driven forward by the firing pin spring; the striker of the firing pin hits the primer of the cartridge, firing the round (Figures 3-16 and 3-17).

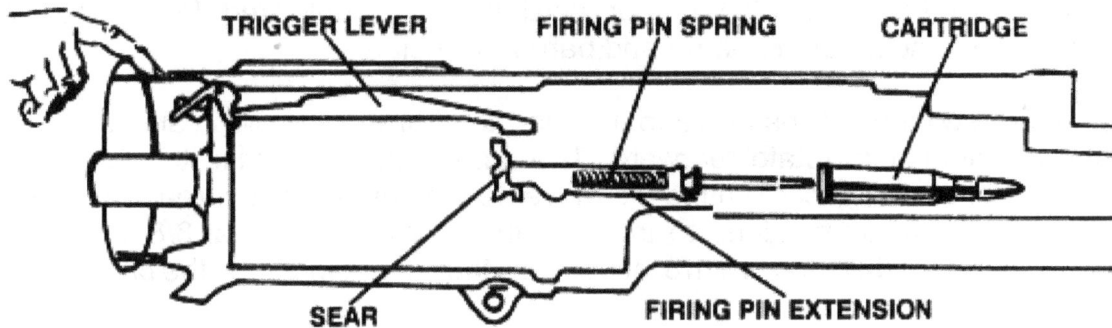

Figure 3-16 Firing – ready to fire

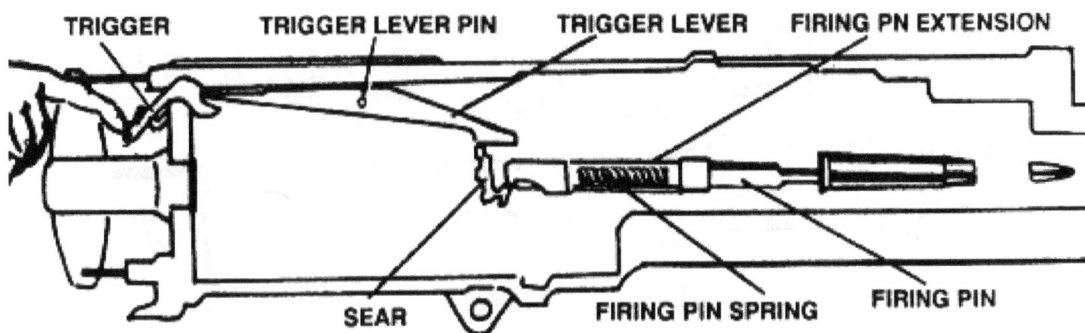

Figure 3-17 Firing – round ignited

(2) For automatic firing, the bolt-latch release must be locked or held depressed so that the bolt latch will not engage the notches in the top of the bolt, holding the bolt to the rear as in single-shot firing. The trigger is pressed and held down. Each time the bolt travels forward in counter-recoil, the trigger lever depresses the sear, releasing the firing pin extension assembly and the firing pin. This automatically fires the next round when the forward movement of the recoiling groups is nearly completed. The gun should fire about 1/16 inch before the recoiling groups are fully forward. Only the first round should be fired with the parts fully forward. The gun fires automatically as long as the trigger and bolt latch are held down and ammunition is fed into the gun.

E. **Unlocking.** The bolt is unlocked from the barrel and barrel extension.

(1) At the instant of firing, the bolt is locked to the barrel extension and against the rear end of the barrel by the breech lock, which is on top of the breech lock cam and in the breech lock recess in the bottom of the bolt. When the cartridge explodes, the bullet travels out of the barrel; the force of recoil drives the recoiling groups rearward. During the first 3/4 inch, the recoiling groups are locked together. As this movement takes place, the breech lock is moved off the breech lock cam stop, allowing the breech lock depressors (acting on the breech lock pin) to force the breech lock down, out of its recess from the bottom of the

bolt. At the end of the first 3/4 inch of recoil, the bolt is unlocked, free to move to the rear independent of the barrel and barrel extension.

(2) As the recoiling groups move to the rear, the barrel extension causes the tips of the accelerator to rotate rearward. The accelerator tips strike the lower rear projection of the bolt, accelerating the movement of the bolt to the rear. The barrel and barrel extension continue to travel to the rear an additional 3/8 inch or an approximate total distance of 1 1/8 inches until they are stopped by the barrel buffer assembly (Figure 3-18).

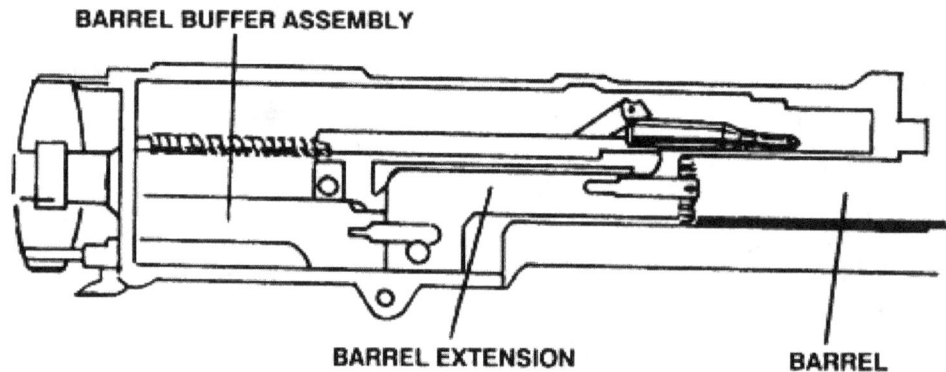

Figure 3-18 Unlocking – barrel and barrel extension stopped by the barrel buffer assembly

(3) During the recoil of 1 1/8 inches, the barrel buffer spring is compressed by the barrel extension shank, since the notch on the shank is engaged in the cross groove in the piston rod head. The spring is locked in the compressed position by the claws of the accelerator, which engage the shoulders of the barrel extension shank. After its initial travel of 3/4 inch, the bolt travels an additional 6 3/8 inches to the rear, after it is unlocked from the barrel and barrel extension, for a total of 7 1/8 inches. During this movement, the driving springs are compressed. The rearward movement of the bolt is stopped as the bolt strikes the buffer plate. Part of the recoil energy of the bolt is stored by the driving
spring rod assembly, and part is absorbed by the buffer disks in the backplate (Figure 3-19).

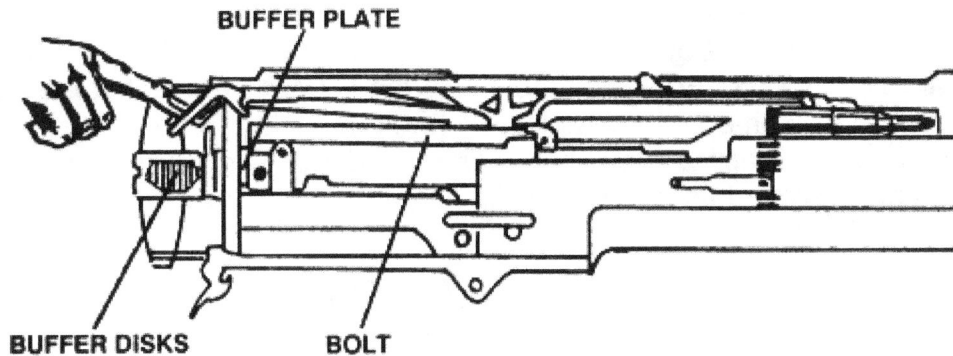

BUFFER PLATE

BUFFER DISKS   **BOLT**

Figure 3-19 Unlocking – recoil movement completed

F. **Extracting.** The empty cartridge case is pulled from the chamber.

(1) The empty case, held by the T-slot, has been expanded by the force of the explosion; therefore, it fits snugly in the chamber. If the case is withdrawn from the chamber too rapidly, it may be torn. To prevent this, and to ensure slow initial extraction of the case, the top forward edge of the breech lock and the forward edge of the lock recess in the bolt are beveled. As the breech lock is unlocked, the initial movement of the bolt away from the barrel and barrel extension is gradual.

(2) The slope of the locking faces facilitates locking and unlocking and prevents sticking. The leverage of the accelerator tips on the bolt speeds extraction after it is started by kicking the bolt to the rear to extract the empty case from the chamber.

G. **Ejecting.** The empty cartridge case is expelled from the receiver.

(1) As the bolt starts its forward movement (counter-recoil), the extractor lug rides below the extractor switch, forcing the extractor assembly farther down until the round is in the center of the T-slot of the bolt.

(2) The round, still gripped by the extractor, ejects the empty case from the T-slot. The last empty case of an ammunition belt is pushed out by the ejector.

H. **Cocking.** The firing pin is withdrawn into the cocked position.

(1) When the recoiling groups are fully forward, the top of the cocking lever rests on the rear half of the V-slot in the top plate bracket. As the bolt moves to the rear, the top of the cocking lever is forced forward. The lower end pivots to the rear on the cocking lever pin. The rounded nose of the cocking lever, which fits through the slot in the firing pin extension, forces the extension to the rear, compressing the firing pin spring against the sear stop pin (accelerator stop). As the firing pin extension is pressed to the rear, the hooked notch of the extension rides over the sear notch, forcing the sear down. The sear spring forces the sear back up after the hooked notch of the firing pin extension has entered the sear notch.

(2) The pressure of the sear and firing pin springs holds the two notches locked together. There is a slight over travel of the firing pin extension in its movement to the rear to ensure proper engagement with the sear. As the bolt starts forward, the over travel is taken up and completed when the cocking lever enters the V-slot of the top plate bracket and is caromed toward the rear; pressure on the cocking lever is relieved as the bolt starts forward.

Operation

The overall operation of the MG includes how to load, unload, and clear the weapon. During the weapon's operation, it is mandatory that all ammunition be free of dirt and corrosion, that the ammunition be properly linked, and that the double-linked end is at the top of the ammunition can.

Operational maintenance checks and services. These are checks that the gunner must perform before he can safely fire the weapon. They are divided into three groups: before, during, and after firing checks.

Operations Checklist

A. <u>Before Firing Checks</u>

(1) Ensure the weapon is in Condition 4.

(2) Check bore and chamber using cleaning rod with swab to remove excessive oil, foreign material, and obstruction.

(3) Check to make sure the barrel support and breech bearing are free of dirt.

(4) Raise the cover.

(5) Check feed mechanism and bolt switch for proper assembly.

(6) Check headspace and timing; if not correct, adjust.

(7) Check the rear sight to ensure it is clean and functioning properly.

(8) Set the rear sight at range of 1,000 yards and windage at 0.

(9) Check the traversing and elevation mechanism to ensure it is securely attached to the receiver.

(10) Ensure traversing handwheel is centered.

(11) Check to ensure elevating screws are equally exposed above and below the elevating handwheel.

(12) Check the backplate and ensure it is latched and locked in place.

(13) Ensure the bolt latch release is locked in the down position by the bolt latch release lock to place gun in automatic mode.

(14) Clean and oil spare parts and tools as well as ensure SL-3 complete.

(15) Inspect ammunition for cleanliness and good condition.

B. <u>During Firing Checks</u>

(1) Maintain lubrication while firing in accordance with lubrication guide.

(2) Observe the function of the gun to anticipate failures.

(3) Watch for bulged cases to prevent a ruptured case; if this occurs, readjust headspace.

(4) Adjust rear sight per fire command.

(5) Ensure ammunition stays correctly aligned with feed way and protect from sun, moisture, and dirt.

(6) Watch for link stoppage.

(7) Make a Condition 4 weapon.

C. <u>After Firing Checks</u>

(1) Ensure the weapon is clear.

(2) Clean the weapon.

(3) Inspect weapon for any damaged or broken parts.

(4) Lightly oil all parts.

LEFT-HAND FEED

By repositioning some of the components, the MG is capable of alternate feed. Ammunition can be fed into the weapon from the right or left side of the receiver; however, the Army uses only left-hand feed (See Table 3-1).

PART	POSITION
Belt-feed lever, shoulder headless pin, and spring.	Upper (rear) hole; lug of feed lever is on left side of cover.
Belt-feed slide.	Feed pawl is on left side of cover.
Belt-feed pawl arm.	Arm toward latch end of cover, pointing right.
Cover latch shaft lever	Left side of cover.
Cartridge stops and link stripper.	Right-hand rear cartridge stop assembly and front cartridge stop on right side of feedway.
Retracting slide with handle.	Right sideplate.
Belt-holding pawl.	Left side of feedway.
Bolt switch.	Cam grove in line with "L" on bolt.

Table 3-1 Position of parts for left-hand feed

Headspace and Timing

Headspace is the distance between the face of the bolt and the base of the cartridge case, fully seated in the chamber. Timing is the adjustment of the gun so that firing takes place when the recoiling parts are in the correct position for firing. Because the cartridge is held by the T-slot of the bolt, headspace with the MG is measured as the distance between the rear of the barrel and the face of the bolt. This space occurs when the recoiling parts are forward and there is positive contact between the breech lock recess in the bolt and the lock in the barrel extensions. Periodic calibration checks should be made of the gauge by direct support personnel at least annually.

WARNING
Firing a weapon that has improperly set headspace and timing could result in damage to the machine gun, or injury to the gunner. Damage may also occur in the trunnion block, base of the barrel, or face of the bolt. This warning applies whether the gun is firing service ammunition or M1E1 blanks. (The weapon has improper early timing when two rounds are fired – and firing stops.)

A. **Gauges.** The headspace and timing gauge consists of a headspace gauge and two timing gauges (Figure 3-20). These gauges provide an accurate means of checking the adjustment of headspace and timing.

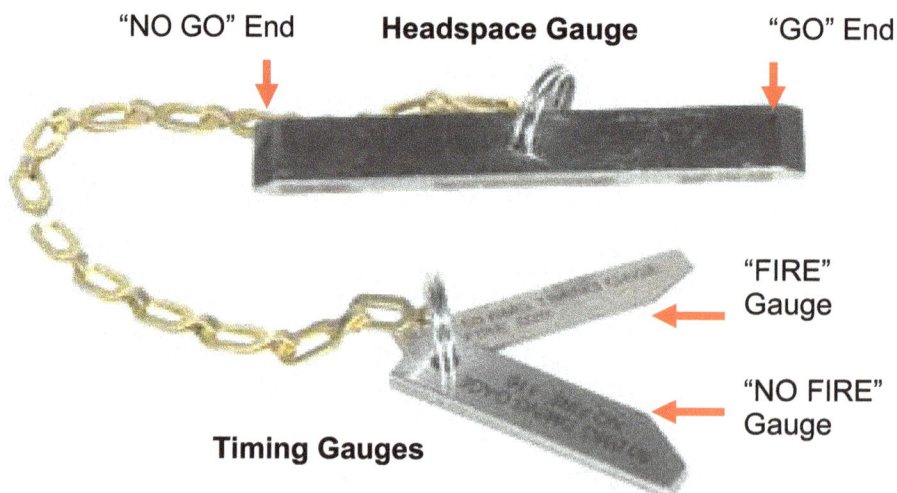

Figure 3-20 Headspace and timing gauge (BH-M2-HSTG)

NOTE- The headspace and timing gauge should be kept with the gun at all times.

B. **Headspace.** Check and set headspace before firing, after assembling the gun, and after replacing the barrel or receiver group. Use the following procedures to set headspace.

Set Headspace and Timing on a Caliber .50 M2 Machine Gun

WARNING- Make sure the gun is clear of ammunition before starting.

A. Adjust headspace.
(1) Raise the cover group all the way up (Figure 3-21).

Figure 3-21 Raising the feedway cover

(2) Grasp the retracting slide handle with your right hand, palm up; pull the bolt to the rear until the barrel-locking spring lug aligns with the 3/8-inch hole in the right side plate of the receiver (Figure 3-22).

Figure 3-22 Retracting the bolt to observe the barrel locking spring lug aligns with the 3/8" hole

(3) Screw the barrel (to the right) fully into the barrel extension; then unscrew the barrel two notches (clicks) (Figure 3-23).

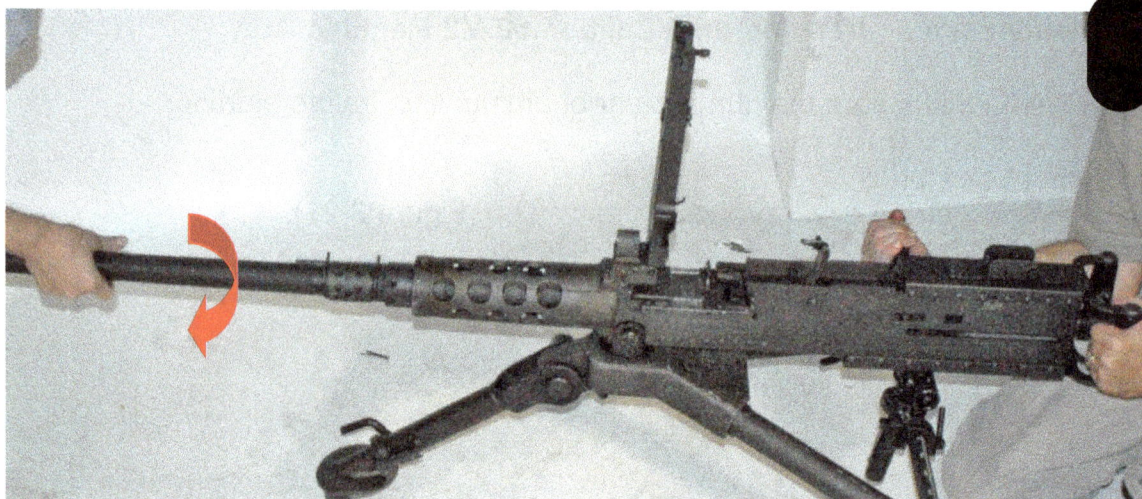

Figure 3-23 Screwing in the barrel

(4) Release the retracting slide handle and allow the bolt to go forward slowly.

WARNING- Check the barrel to make sure it is locked in the forward position. Try to turn the barrel in either direction. The barrel should not turn. If it does, stop and notify your supervisor or unit armorer at once. DO NOT try to fire the gun.

(5) Ensure the weapon is in single-shot mode. Pull the bolt to the rear and hold it; then press the bolt-latch release, and allow the bolt to go forward slowly. DO NOT fire the weapon.

(6) Pull the retracting slide handle back until the barrel extension separates (not more than 1/16 of an inch) from the trunnion block. Make sure the GO/NO GO gauge has no broken, bent, rusted, or pitted areas, or other defects that could affect the weapon's dimensional tolerances.

(7) Raise the cartridge extractor to the rear. Try to insert each end of the GO/NO-GO headspace gauge in the T-slot between the face of the bolt and the rear of the barrel (Figures 3-24a & 3-24b).

Figure 3-24a NO GO end of gauge   **Figure 3-24b GO end of gauge**

a. IF the GO end of the gauge enters freely up to the ring on the center of the gauge, and the NO GO end will not enter, the headspace is set correctly.

b. If the GO end of the gauge will not enter the T-slot freely, adjust the headspace as follows:

(a) Retract the bolt with the retracting handle so you can see the barrel-locking lug spring in the center of the receiver hole on the right side of the receiver (Figure 2).

(b) Unscrew the barrel from the barrel extension one notch (click) at a time; until the GO end of the gauge enters the T-slot freely (check after each click). To complete the adjustment, try to insert the NO-GO end of the gauge. If it will not enter the T-slot, the headspace is set correctly.

c. If the NO GO end of the gauge enters the T-slot, adjust as follows:

(a) Retract the bolt with the retracting handle so you can see the barrel-locking lug spring in center of receiver hole on right side of receiver (Figure 2).

(b) Screw the barrel into the barrel extension one notch (click) at a time, until the NO GO end of the gauge will not enter the T-slot (check after each click). To complete the adjustment, try to insert the GO end of the gauge. If it inserts into the T-slot easily, the headspace is set correctly.

CAUTION: After you have corrected the headspace, recheck the barrel's positive locking action by trying to screw it in or out with the bolt in the forward position. If you can do either, then DO NOT fire the machine gun. Notify your supervisor or the unit armorer.

B. Check and adjust timing.

(1) Check timing.

a. Make sure you have set the headspace correctly.

b. Pull the bolt to the rear with the retracting slide to cock the machine gun. While holding the handle to the rear, depress the bolt latch release, and allow the bolt to go forward slowly. DO NOT press the trigger.

c. Retract the bolt just enough (1/16 of an inch) to insert the NO-FIRE gauge between the barrel extension and trunnion block, with the beveled edge of the gauge against the notches in the barrel. Release the retracting slide handle slowly (Figures 3-25a & 3-25b).

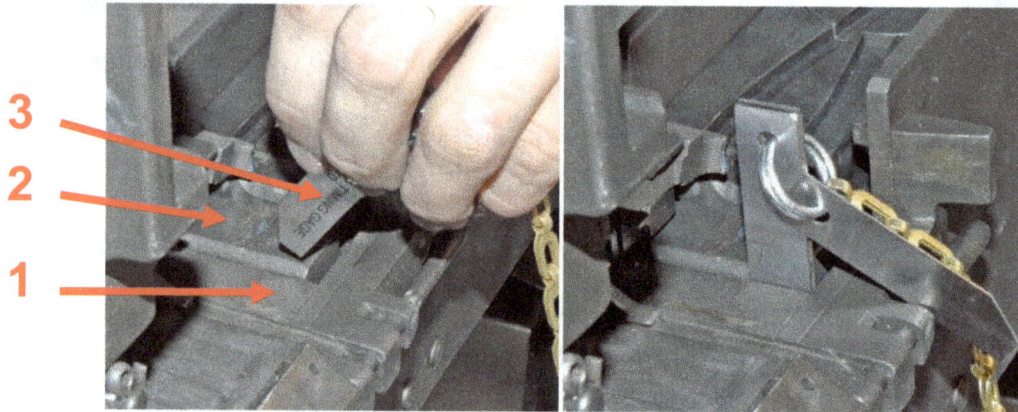

Figure 3-25a   **Figure 3-25b**
NO GO gauge positioning
(bevel against barrel notches)

1 – Trunnion Block   **3 – NO FIRE Gauge**
2 – Barrel Extension

d. Depress the trigger (Figure 3-26). The gun should not fire. If it does not, continue the timing check. However, if it does fire, go to Step 2b.

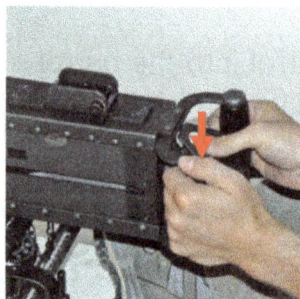

Figure 3-26 Depressing the trigger

e. Grasp the retracting slide handle. Retract the bolt just enough (1/16th of an inch) to remove the NO-FIRE gauge. Insert the FIRE gauge between the barrel extension and trunnion block, with the beveled edge of the gauge against the notches in the barrel (Figure 3-27). Release the retracting slide handle slowly.

Figure 3-27 FIRE gauge positioning
(bevel against barrel notches)

1 – Trunnion Block	**3 – FIRE Gauge**
2 – Barrel Extension	**4 – NO FIRE Gauge**

f. Depress the trigger (Figure 3-26). The gun should fire. If it does not, go to Step 2b.

(2) Adjust timing.

a. Remove the gauge.

b. Pull the bolt to the rear with the retracting slide to cock machine gun. Press the bolt-catch release, and allow the bolt to go forward slowly. DO NOT press the trigger.

c. Grasp the retracting slide handle. Retract the bolt just enough to insert the FIRE gauge between the barrel extension and the trunnion block, with the beveled edge of the gauge against the notches in the barrel (Figure 3-27).

WARNING- DO NOT remove the backplate unless the bolt is in the forward position. Never cock the gun with the backplate off. Stand to one side of the weapon when removing the backplate to avoid possible injury from the driving spring rod.

d. Move to the side of the gun and remove the backplate.

e. Screw the timing adjustment nut all the way down (to the left). The nut should turn hard (Figure 3-28).

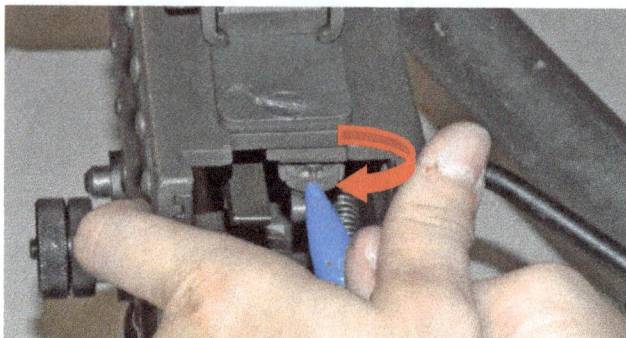

Figure 3-28 Adjusting Timing (Rotate timing adjustment nut to the left)

f. Try to fire by pushing firmly up on the trigger lever (Figure 3-29). The gun should not fire.

Figure 3-29 Depressing the trigger lever

g. Screw the timing adjustment nut up (to the right), one click at a time. Push up firmly on the trigger lever after each click. **Repeat until the gun fires**.

h. Turn the timing adjustment nut up (to the right), **two more clicks**. DO NOT turn the timing adjustment nut any more (there is a five click range – two clicks places the timing in the middle of this range).

i. Remove the FIRE gauge, and replace the backplate.

j. Recheck timing with the FIRE/NO FIRE gauge __twice__ more to confirm that the adjustment is correct.

Field Expedient Methods. When a go/no go gauge is not available, you can still set the headspace and timing using field expedient methods. However, this method should be used only in combat.

A. *To set headspace:*

1) Raise the cover and retract the bolt in the normal manner until the barrel-locking-spring lug is centered in the 3/8-inch hole on the right side of the receiver.
2) Hold the bolt in this position and screw the barrel fully into the barrel extension; then unscrew the barrel two clicks or notches.

B. *To set timing:*

1) Use a dog tag or a dime as a FIRE gauge.
2) Use a nickel and a dime or four dog tags as a NO FIRE gauge.
3) Set the timing using the normal procedure.

C. *To check for correct settings:*

1) Attempt to fire the weapon. If it fires sluggishly, clear the weapon, and then unscrew the barrel one more notch.
2) Recheck the rate of fire. Repeat the procedures in the paragraph; however, do not exceed two more clicks.
3) Do not unscrew the barrel more than one notch between firings.

Tripod Operations

Setting up and mounting the .50 BMG on the tripod

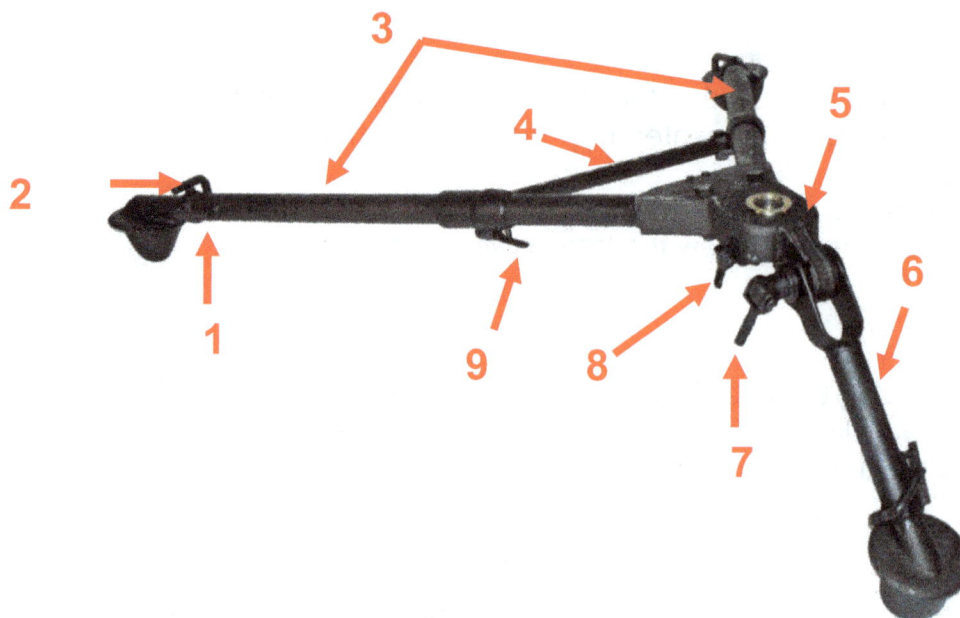

Figure 3-30 M3 tripod mount

1 – Indexing Lever Assembly
2 – Leg Clamping Handle
3 – Trail Legs
4 – Traversing Bar
5 – Tripod Head

6 – Front Leg
7 – Front Leg Clamp Handle
8 – Pintle Lock Release Cam
9 – Rear Right Leg Sliding Sleeve

Tripod Mount, M3. The M3 mount is the standard ground mount of the caliber .50 machine gun (Figure 3-30). It is a folding tripod with three telescopic tubular legs connected at the tripod head. Each leg ends in a metal shoe that can be stamped into the ground for greater stability. The two trail legs are joined together by the traversing bar. The traversing bar serves as a support for the traversing and elevating mechanism, which in turn supports the rear of the gun. The tripod head furnishes a front support for the mounted gun that is further supported by the short front leg. When the tripod is emplaced on flat terrain with all extensions closed, the adjustable front leg should form an angle of about 60 degrees with the ground. This places the gun on a low mount about 12 inches above the ground. To raise the tripod farther off the ground, extend the telescopic front and trail legs enough to keep the tripod level and maintain the stability of the mount.

(1) To set the tripod trail legs:
    (a) Unscrew the leg-clamping handle, press down on the indexing lever, and extend the leg to the desired length.
    (b) Align the indexing lever stud with one of the holes in the tripod leg extension.

(c) Release the pressure on the indexing lever, allowing the stud to fit the desired hole. Tighten the leg-clamping handle.

(2) *To set the front leg of the tripod:*
    (a) Turn the front leg-clamp handle counterclockwise to loosen the front leg.
    (b) Adjust the leg to the desired angle and tighten the front leg clamp.

(3) To secure the tripod legs, stamp the metal shoe on each tripod leg into the ground. Sandbag each leg to stabilize the M2 for firing.

Firing Positions

The **tripod firing positions** are prone, sitting, and standing. They are assumed in the following manner:

1. The **prone position** (Figure 3-31) is used when firing from the tripod that is set in a low position. It is assumed by lying on the ground directly behind the gun. The gunner then spreads his legs a comfortable distance apart with his toes turned outward. His left elbow rests on the ground, and his left hand grasps the elevating handwheel of the T&E. His right hand lightly grasps the right spade grip with his right thumb in a position to press the trigger. The position of his body can then be adjusted to position his firing eye in alignment with the sights of the weapon.

Figure 3-31 Prone firing position

2. The **sitting position** (Figure 3-32) can be used when the tripod is set in a high or low position. The gunner sits directly behind the gun between the legs of the tripod. He may extend his legs under the tripod or cross them, depending on his physique. The gunner then places both elbows on the inside of his thighs to get the best support. He grasps the elevating handwheel of the T&E with the left hand, and lightly grasps the right spade grip with his right hand. He must ensure that the right thumb is in position to press the trigger

Figure 3-32 Sitting firing position

3. The **standing position** (Figure 3-33) is used when the gunner is firing from a fighting position. This position is assumed by standing directly behind the gun with the feet spread a comfortable distance apart. The gunner grasps the elevating handwheel of the T&E with the left hand. He lightly grasps the right spade grip with the right hand, ensuring that the right thumb is in a position to press the trigger. Adjustment of the body is allowed in order to align the firing eye with the sights on the weapon

Figure 3-33 Standing firing position

Range Setting and Laying

Range setting and laying the gun are important elements in marksmanship training. It is this training that prepares the gunner to place fire accurately and rapidly on his target in combat. To set ranges properly, the gunner must be trained in rear sight operation.

A. Setting ranges on the rear sight is a simple but important task. The gunner just has to rotate the elevating screw knob in a clockwise manner to move the peep sight up or counterclockwise to move it down. The range scale on the left is graduated in mils and the scale on the right in yards. The gunner must align the hairline index of the peep sight with the scale index line at the desired range as quickly and accurately as possible.

B. Laying is placing the barrel of the weapon on a direct line with the target using the sights. This procedure must also be done as quickly and accurately as possible.

C. The range setting and laying exercises are designed to require the gunner to practice and the instructor to evaluate both correct sight alignments and correct placements of aiming points. The exercise starts with the gunner in the sitting firing position with the rear sight down. The coach will announce a range and general aiming point. The gunner will repeat the range and direction of target. The coach will then announce, "Begin." The gunner will raise and set his sights and align the weapon on the aim point. When the gunner completes this task, he will announce "Up." The coach will then get behind the weapon and check the range setting and aim point and critique the gunner on his findings. This exercise will be continued until speed and accuracy are obtained.

Traversing and Elevating Mechanism

Manipulation of the T&E mechanism (Figure 3-34) is another key factor in effectively engaging targets. The gunner is taught how to manipulate the T&E mechanism instinctively to shift from one target to another. The gunners are trained to use the traversing handwheel, the traversing slide lock, and the elevating handwheel.

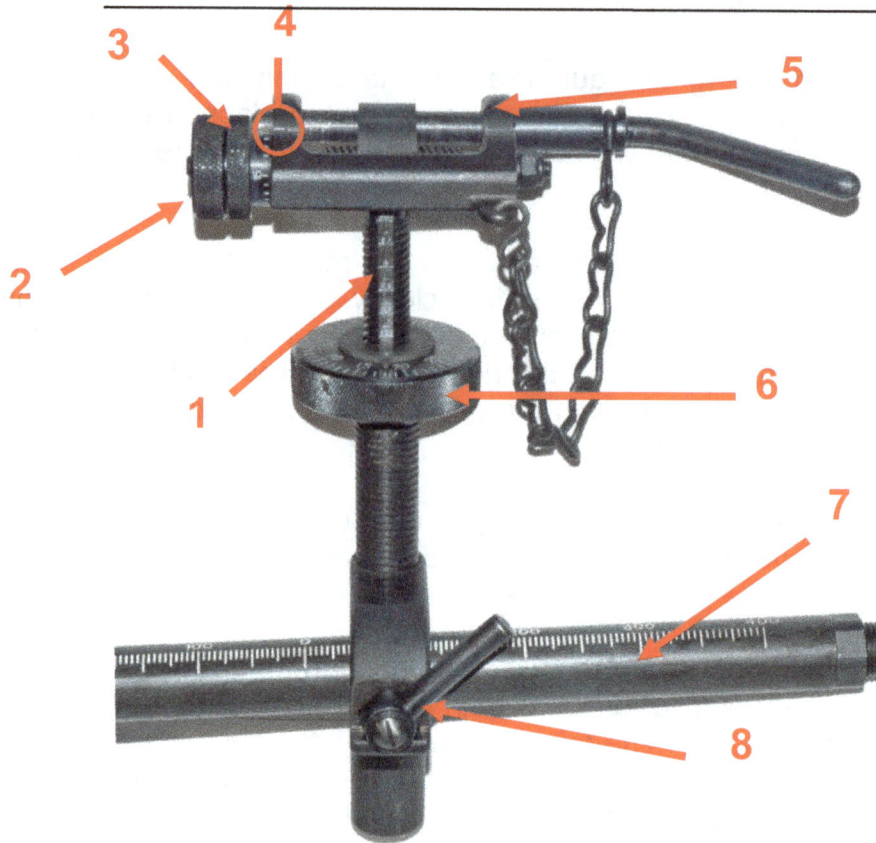

Figure 3-34 Traversing and elevating mechanism

1 – Elevation Screw Scale Plate	5 – Yoke
2 – Traversing Handwheel	6 – Elevation Handwheel
3 – Locking Nut	7 – Traversing Bar
4 – Scale	8 – Traversing Bar Lock

A. The traversing mechanism consists of a traversing handwheel, locking nut, scale, and yoke. The T&E mechanism is attached to the traversing bar of the M3 bipod.

(1) The traversing bar is graduated in 5-mil increments and fits between the trail legs of the M3 tripod. The traversing slide and screw assembly are clamped in place on the traversing bar by the traversing slide lock lever. When the traversing slide is locked to the traversing bar, the traversing handwheel should be centered. The traversing slide is properly mounted when the lock lever is to the rear and the traversing handwheel is positioned to the left.

(2) To make changes in direction, loosen the traversing slide lock lever and move the slide along the traversing bar. This adjustment permits traverse of 400 mils left or right of the zero index in the center of the traversing bar. Readings on the traversing bar are taken from the left side of the traversing slide. For changes of 50 mils or less in deflection, turn the traversing

handwheel. This action allows a traverse of 50 mils left or right of center. One click in the traversing handwheel signifies 1 mil change in direction.

B. The elevating mechanism consists of an upper and lower elevating screw, which is connected to the gun by inserting the quick-release pin assembly through the holes in the upper elevating screw yoke and the rear mounting lugs of the receiver. A scale, graduated in mils, is fitted to the upper screw to indicate elevation. This scale is marked to show (-) minus 250 mils in depression and (+) plus 100 mils in elevation from the zero setting.

C. The elevating handwheel is graduated in 1-mil increments from 0 to 50 mils and is fastened to the elevating screw by a screw lock. This arrangement synchronizes the handwheel graduations with those on the upper elevating screw. A spring-actuated index device produces a clicking sound when the handwheel is turned. Each click equals 1 mil change in elevation. The handwheel is turned clockwise to depress the barrel and counterclockwise to elevate.

D. Direction and elevation readings constitute the data necessary to engage preselected target areas during limited visibility. These readings are measured by and recorded from the traversing bar and the T&E mechanism. To obtain accurate readings, the T&E must be first zeroed, with all measurements recorded in mils.

(1) To zero the traversing handwheel, the gunner must first hold the T&E so that the traversing handwheel is on his left as he looks at it. He then turns the handwheel toward himself until it stops, loosens the locking nut slightly, and aligns the zero on the scale with the zero on the elevating screw yoke. Once the zeros are aligned, he tightens the locking nut. He must then turn the handwheel two complete turns away from the body and stop. The scale should again be on the zero. If this procedure is done at night, the gunner will turn 50 clicks away from him.

(2) To zero the elevating handwheel, the gunner must first turn the handwheel up or down until the handwheel is level with the line directly under the zero on the elevating screw plate scale, and the elevating handwheel indicator is pointing to the zero on the top of the handwheel. The elevating mechanism sleeve is then rotated up until it is stopped by the handwheel. The gunner rotates the sleeve down until it stops, making sure he counted each complete rotation. He divides the number of rotations by two, rotates the sleeve back up that number, and stops. The T&E mechanism is now ready to be attached to the tripod.

(3) To obtain and record direction readings, the gunner sets the sight on the proper range to hit the target, loosens the traversing slide lock lever, and slides the T&E mechanism along the traversing bar until the weapon is sighted on the aiming point of the target. The T&E mechanism is then locked down by tightening the traversing slide lock lever. All readings are taken

from the left side of the sleeve mechanism. If the left side of the sleeve is not exactly on one of the 5-mil tick marks, the gunner must slide the sleeve to the next smaller tick mark to align it exactly. The traversing handwheel is then used to move the weapon back on point of aim. The direction is now ready to be recorded. The reading is taken from the number on the traversing bar and the direction from the direction of the barrel of the weapon. If the sleeve mechanism is on the right side of the zero on the traversing bar, then the reading is left; if it is on the left side of the zero, then it is a right reading. The width of a target may also be measured and recorded by first moving the traversing handwheel until the sights are aligned with the right or left side of the target. The clicks required to do this measure the width.

NOTE: Before repositioning the weapon for another target, the gunner must realign the handwheel.

(4) To obtain an elevation reading, the gunner must first ensure that the sights are aligned and at the desired aim point of the target. The elevation reading is made up of two portions, a major reading and a minor reading. The major reading is taken from the elevating screw plate scale. The scale is graduated in 50-mil increments and ranges from a minus. (-) 250 mils to a plus (+) 100 mils with a zero between them. There is an index line below each number and a plus or minus. sign above each number, with the exception of the zero. The zero does not have a plus or minus sign. To obtain the elevation reading, the gunner should lower his head until his eyes are level with the elevating handwheel. The major reading is the first number with a plus or minus sign, with its index line just visible above the elevating handwheel. The minor reading is taken from the top surface of the elevating handwheel. It is graduated in l-mil increments for a total of 50 mils. The handwheel is also equipped with an indicator that points to each number on the handwheel as it is turned. Once the gunner has the major reading from the screw plate scale, he will then get the minor reading by looking at the number at which the indicator is pointing. Both portions of the elevation reading are recorded by placing a slash (/) mark between the two portions.

(5) An elevation reading is valid only on one T&E mechanism. If the same data is placed on another T&E mechanism using the same weapon, the data may be inaccurate. The number of threads exposed on the T&E must remain the same; both when obtaining and recording data. If the number of exposed threads is changed in any manner, the firing will be off target. For example, when a gun is freed to engage targets in the secondary sector, the data will be correct if the gunner ensures that the same amount of threads is exposed when he returns to his primary sector of fire.

(6) To ensure that the data is correct, the gunner should fire and adjust his weapon.

E. The T&E manipulation exercise gives the gunner practice and the instructor a tool to evaluate the gunner's progress (Figure 3-35). The exercise is conducted in two stages. Both stages require the coach to give directions and the gunner to respond. In the first stage, the coach positions himself about 10 paces to the front of the gun. He then directs the gunner to manipulate the weapon in certain directions. He indicates the direction by the use of hand signals. The gunner responds by manipulating the T&E mechanism with his left hand. The gunner must keep his eyes on the coach; at no time during this exercise is he permitted to look at the T&E mechanism. The coach must be very attentive during the first stage because the gunner will be manipulating using the elevating handwheel and the traversing handwheel. The second stage is done in the same way, except the gunner must make bold changes in elevation and deflection. The exercise continues until the instructor is satisfied that the gunner can manipulate the weapon by T&E without looking at the device. This exercise can also be conducted using the basic MG target. The gunner will be shifted from one selected target to another. The coach must observe all movements of the gunner during this training.

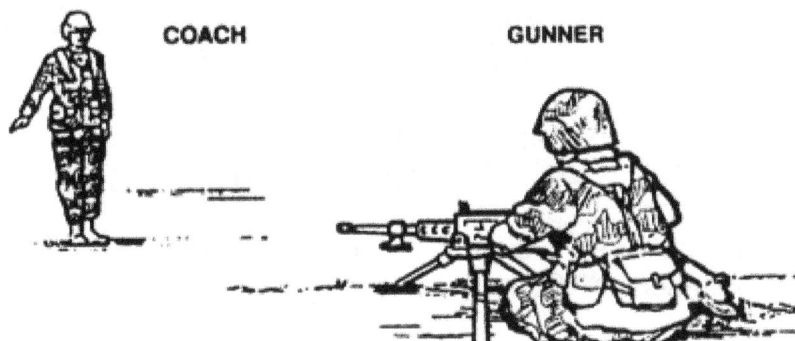

COACH   GUNNER

Figure 3-35 Manipulation Drill

Range Determination

Range determination is the process of estimating the distance to a target from a gunner's position. The ability of the gunner to get the range to, sight on, and destroy a target is the realism of combat. Under combat conditions, ranges are seldom known in advance; therefore, the effectiveness of fire depends largely upon the accuracy and speed of the gunner in determining range. Some methods of determining range are estimating by eye (Table 3-2), firing the gun, measuring range from a map or aerial photograph, stepping off the distance, or securing information from other units. Ranges are determined to the nearest 100 meters for machine-gun firing. In combat, the most commonly used methods are estimating by eye and firing the gun. There is also a method used for measuring lateral distance.

FACTOR	APPEARS NEARER (Range is underestimated when) —	APPEARS MORE DISTANT (Range is overestimated when) —
Target visibility.	Most of the target is visible and offers a clear outline.	Only a small part of the target is seen or target is small in relation to its surroundings.
Terrain, or position of the observer.	Looking across a depression, most of which is hidden from view. Looking down from high ground. Looking down a straight, open road or along a railroad track. Looking over uniform surfaces such as water, snow, desert, or grain fields.	Looking across a depression, all of which is visible. Looking from low toward high ground. When vision is narrowly confined as in streets, draws, or forest trails.
Light and atmosphere	In bright light or the sun is shining from behind the observer. The target is in sharp contrast with the background, or is silhouetted by reason of size, shape, or color, or is seen in the clear atmosphere of high altitudes.	In poor light such as dawn and dusk, in rain, snow, fog, or when the sun is in the observer's eyes. The target blends into the background or terrain.

Figure 3-2 Factors affecting range estimation by eye

A. The two techniques of eye estimation are the 100-meter unit of measure method and the appearance of objects method.

(1) When using the 100-meter unit of measure method, the gunner must be able to visualize what 100 meters looks like on the ground. With this distance in mind, the gunner can mentally determine the number of 100-meter units between his position and the target. The accuracy of this method is limited to 500 meters or less, and it requires constant practice (Figure 3-36).

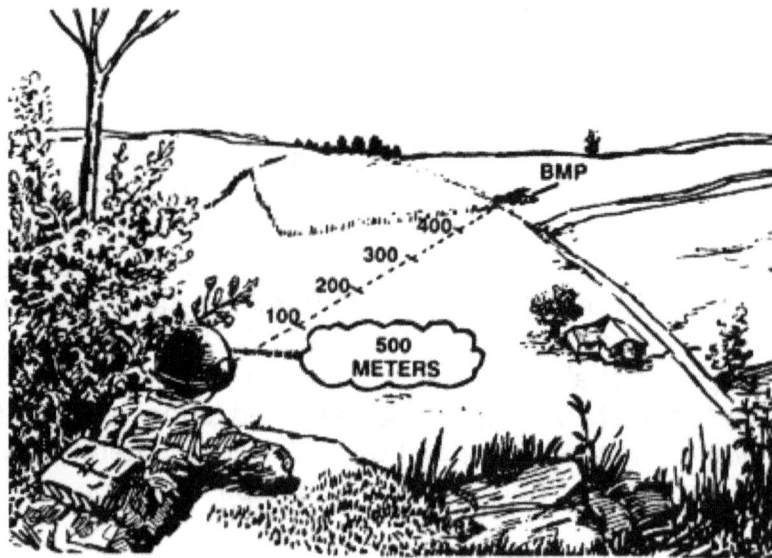

Figure 3-36 100-meter unit of measure method, less than 500 meters

(2) For targets that appear to be more than 500 meters away, the gunner must modify this technique. The gunner selects what he thinks is the halfway point between the target and his position. He then mentally counts the number of 100-meter units to the halfway point and doubles it. This method of range determination is not accurate beyond 1,000 meters (Figure 3-37).

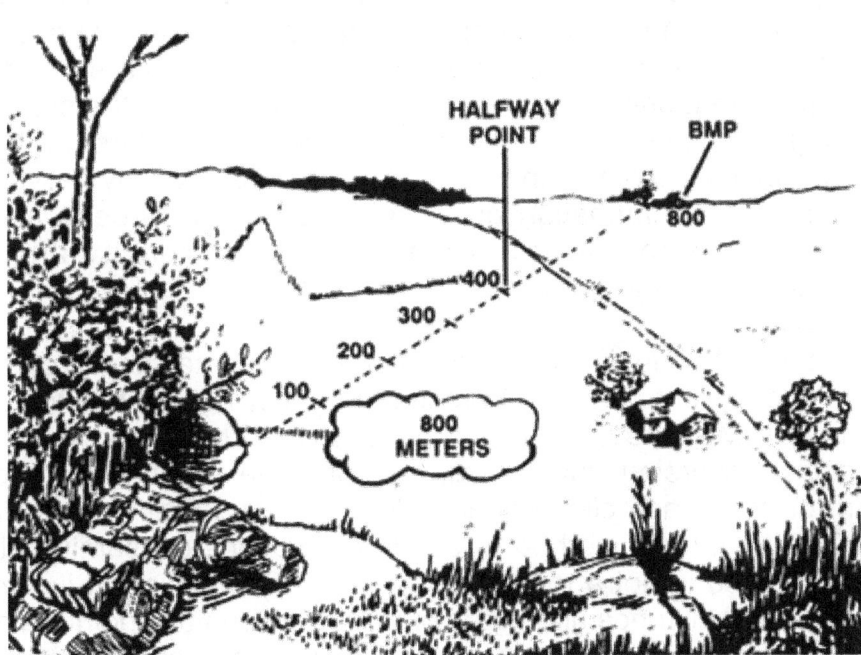

Figure 3-37 100-meter unit of measure method, more than 50 meters

(3) Some terrains affect the appearance of 100-meter units of measure. When the terrain slopes upward toward the target, 100 meters appears longer than on level terrain. It appears shorter on downward sloping terrain. The gunner must consider these two factors when using the 100-meter unit of measure method.

(4) The appearance of objects method may be used if the gunner is unable to use the 100-meter unit of measure method because of terrain. To use this method, the gunner learns through practice how familiar objects look at various known ranges. This can be achieved by studying the appearance of a man standing 100 meters away. The gunner must then fix the appearance of the man firmly in his mind to include the size and details of his uniform and equipment. Next, he studies the same man at the same distance in the kneeling and prone positions. This procedure is used at 200, 300, 400, and 500 meters. By comparing the appearance of the man at these known ranges, he can establish a series of mental images that will help him determine range on unfamiliar terrain out to 500 meters. This

training could also be conducted to familiarize the gunner with other objects, such as weapons and vehicles, at various ranges.

B. Firing the gun is another method of determining range. In this method, the gunner opens fire on the target at the estimated range and moves the center of the beaten zone into the center base of the target by means of the T&E handwheels. He resets the sight so the new line of aim is at the center base of the target and notes the range setting on the rear sight. This range setting may apply only to this gun. When the ground in the vicinity of the target does not permit observation of the strike of the rounds, or when surprise fire on the target is desired, fire is adjusted on a point that offers observation and is known to be the same range as the target. The gunner then lays his gun on the target when ordered. When moving into position occupied by other units, range cards prepared by those units can furnish valuable range information on targets, suspected targets, and various. terrain features. When the tactical situation and time permit, range may be determined by pacing off the distance.

C. Lateral distance measure is a method that the gunner may use to determine the distance from one target to another from left to right or right to left. When the gun is mounted on the M3 tripod, width can be measured by aiming on a point and manipulating the traversing handwheel, counting the clicks from one point to another point of aim. Each click equals one meter at 1,000 meters or one-half meter at 500 meters. This method is accurate but time-consuming. The finger measurement method is not a method of range determination; it is a method of measuring the lateral distance (in fingers or mils) between two points. To measure the distance in fingers between a reference point and a target, extend the arm with palm outward, the fingers cupped, and elbow locked. Close one eye, raise the index finger, and sight along its edge, placing the edge of the finger along the flank of the target or reference point (Figure 3-38). The remaining space is then filled in by raising fingers until the space is covered. The measurement is then stated as being one or more fingers or so many mils, depending on the number of fingers used (Figure 3-39).

Figure 3-38 Index finger aligned

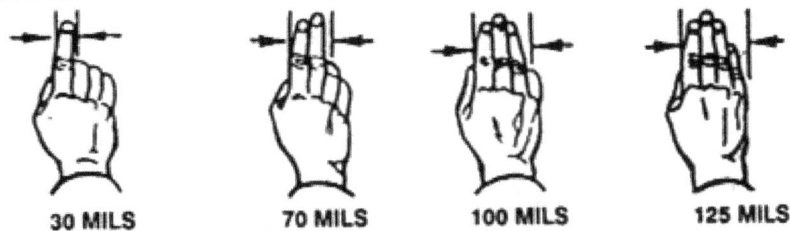

Figure 3-39 Mil/finger relationships

Observation and Adjustment of Fire

The purpose of observation and adjustment of fire practice is to teach the adjustment of fire by observing the strike of the bullets and the flight of the tracers, or by frequent re-laying on the target using sights.

A. Observation is used when firing on the 10-meter range because the impact of the round is visible on the target. When firing at greater distances, the strike of the round on the ground may cause dust to rise that is visible to the gunner; however, during wet weather, the strike cannot always be seen. In this case, use tracer ammunition that allows the gunner or crew to note the strike of the burst in relation to the target.

B. Adjustments on the target can be made using the mil relation; that is, one click of traversing or elevating handwheel moves the strike of the round one-half inch on the target at 10 meters. When firing on field targets, adjustment is made by moving the burst into the target. One click of traverse will move the strike of the round one-half meter at 500 meters, or one meter at 1,000 meters (Figure 3-40). However, the distance one click of elevation will move the strike of the round depends on the range to the target and the slope of the ground. The gunner determines the number of mils necessary to move the center of the strike into the target, and he manipulates the gun the required number of mils. This approach does not require the use of sights. For example, should the gunner fire on a target at 500 meters and observe the strike 10 meters to the right of the target and short about 50 meters, he would traverse the gun to the left 20 clicks (mils) and add one or more clicks (mils), depending on the slope.

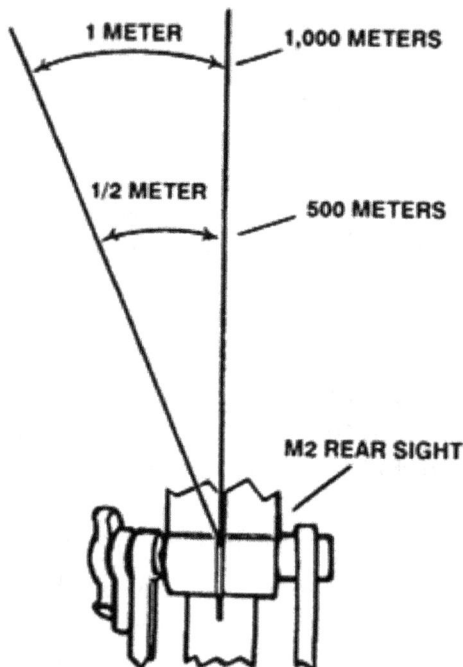

Figure 3-40 Mil relation

C. The gunner may use the adjusted aiming point method to adjust the fire. In this method, the gunner must use his sights. He selects an aiming point that will place the next burst on target. For example, when the gunner fires on a target at 500 meters and estimates that the rounds impacted 20 meters short and 10 meters to the right, he would rapidly select an aiming point about 20 meters beyond the target and 10 meters to the left of it and lay on that aiming point and fire (Figure 3-41).

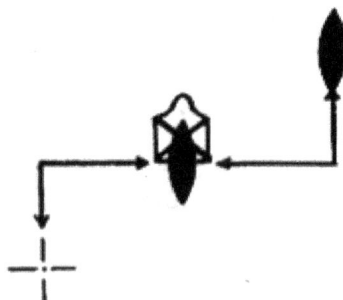

Figure 3-41 Adjusting aiming point method of fire adjustment

Fire Commands

Fire commands are technical instructions issued by a leader to enable the unit or crew to accomplish a desired fire mission. Fire commands have been standardized for infantry direct-fire weapons, and they follow the same sequence. There are two types -- initial fire commands, issued to engage a target, and subsequent fire commands, which are issued to adjust fire, change the rate of fire, interrupt fire, shift fire to a new target, or to terminate the alert. A correct fire command is one that is as brief as clarity permits and yet includes all the elements necessary for the accomplishment of the fire mission. It is given in the proper sequence, transmitted clearly at a rate that permits receipt and application of instructions without confusion.

A. **Elements of the Initial Fire Command.** There are six essential elements of the initial fire command for the machine gun, which are given or implied by using one or more of the methods of control. During training, the gun crew repeats each element as it is given. This repetition is done to avoid confusion and to train the crew to think and act in the proper sequence. The six elements are the alert, direction, description, range, method of fire, and the command to open fire.

(1) *Alert.* This element brings the crew to a state of readiness to receive further instructions. Once alerted, the gunner ensures the gun is loaded. The assistant gunner continuously checks with the leader for orders or instructions and passes them on to the gunner. The oral alert is announced as FIRE MISSION. At this command, the gunners are alerted that a target has been detected and fire may be delivered upon it. When the leader announces the alert, such as FIRE MISSION, both gun crews react to the alert. If only a certain gun is to engage, the leader announces NUMBER 1 (or 2). The other crew follows the fire mission, loads, and lays on the target to take up the fire, if required.

(2) *Direction.* This element indicates the general direction to the target and may be given in one or a combination of the following ways:

(a) The leader gives the direction orally to the target in relation to the position of the gun(s). For example, FRONT, RIGHT FRONT, LEFT FRONT.

(b) The leader can designate a small or obscure target by pointing with his arm and hand or aiming the machine gun. When pointing with his arm and hand, a man standing behind him should be able to look over his shoulder and sight along his arm and index finger to locate the target. When a gun has been aimed at a target, a soldier looking through the sights should be able to see the target.

(c) Tracer ammunition is a quick and sure method of designating a target that is not clearly visible. When using this method, the leader should first give the general direction to direct the gun crew's attention to the desired area. To minimize the loss of surprise when using tracer ammunition, the leader does not fire until he has given all the elements of the fire command except the command to fire. The leader may use his individual weapon or fire one or more bursts from the machine gun. The firing of the tracer(s) then becomes the last element of the fire command and is the signal to open fire.

For example:
FIRE MISSION.
FRONT.
BUNKER.
WATCH MY TRACER(S).
SLOW (or SINGLE SHOT).
The leader fires his individual weapon or a machine gun at the enemy bunker, and then his gun crew(s) open fire.

(d) Another method of designating obscure targets is by using easily recognizable reference points. Prominent terrain features and man-made objects make good reference points. All leaders and members of the crew(s) must be familiar with the terrain features and the terminology used to describe them. The general direction to the reference point should be given.

For example:
FIRE MISSION, NUMBER 2.
FRONT.
REFERENCE: LONE PINE TREE.
TARGET: TRUCK.
Sometimes a target must be designated by using successive reference points.

For example:
FIRE MISSION, NUMBER 1.
RIGHT FRONT.
REFERENCE: RED-ROOFED HOUSE, LEFT TO HAYSTACK,
LEFT TO BARN.
TARGET: MACHINE GUN.

Finger measurements can be used to direct the gun crew's attention to the right or left of reference points. For example:
FIRE MISSION.
LEFT FRONT.
REFERENCE: CROSSROAD. RIGHT FOUR FINGERS.
TARGET: LINE OF TROOPS.

When the guns are mounted on tripods, lateral distance from reference can be accurately announced. When gunners are firing the tripod-mounted gun, lateral distance is assumed to be in mils unless otherwise indicated, so the word "mils" is not necessary.

For example:
FIRE MISSION.
FRONT.
REFERENCE: KNOCKED-OUT TANK. LEFT FOUR ZERO.
TARGET: COLUMN OF TROOPS.

(3) *Description.* The target description is used to create a picture of the target in the minds of the gun crew. The gun crew must know the type of target they are to engage to apply their fire properly. The leader should describe it briefly but accurately.

For example:

Dismounted enemy personnel	TROOPS
Automatic weapons	MACHINE GUN
Armored vehicles	TANK
Artillery or antitank weapon	ANTITANK
Airplanes or helicopters	AIRCRAFT

If the target is obvious, no description is necessary. Finger measurements or mil measurements can be used to designate the width of a linear target when the flanks cannot be pinpointed.

(4) *Range.* The range to the target is given so the gun crew knows how far to look for the target and immediately knows what range setting to place on the rear sight. Range is determined and announced in meters. Since the meter is the standard unit of range measurement, the word "meters" is not announced. With machine guns, the range is determined and announced in even hundreds and thousands. For example: THREE HUNDRED, ONE THOUSAND, ONE ONE HUNDRED. This element may be omitted when the gunners can obviously determine the range; however, it is desirable in some situations to announce the range.

(5) *Method of fire.* This element includes manipulation and rate of fire.

(a) Manipulation is used to prescribe the class of fire with respect to the gun. It is announced FIXED, TRAVERSE, SEARCH, TRAVERSE AND SEARCH, SWINGING TRAVERSE, or FREE GUN.

(b) To control the rate of fire, the gunner may use single shot, slow, rapid, or cyclic.

o Single shot. Place the gun in the single-shot mode and engage the target with aimed shots. The MG is accurate out to 1,500 meters.

o Slow fire. Slow fire consists of less than 40 rounds per minute, in bursts of five to seven rounds, fired at 10- to 15-second intervals.

o Rapid fire. Rapid fire consists of more than 40 rounds per minute, fired in bursts of five to seven rounds, at 5- to 10-second intervals.

o Cyclic fire. Cyclic fire is when the weapon fires 450 to 550 rounds per minute.

(6) *Command to open fire.* If surprise fire is not desired, the command FIRE is given without pause. It is often important that machine gun fire be withheld for maximum effect of surprise fire. To ensure this, the leader may preface the command to commence firing with the words AT MY COMMAND or AT MY SIGNAL. When the gunner(s) is ready to engage the target, they report UP to the assistant gunner(s), who signals they are READY to the leader.

For example:
FIRE MISSION.
FRONT.
TROOPS.
AT MY COMMAND. (Pause until crew members are ready and fire is desired.)
FIRE (or appropriate arm-and-hand signal).

When the leader makes a mistake in the initial fire command, he corrects it by announcing CORRECTION, and then gives the corrected element(s). For example:
FIRE MISSION.
FRONT.
TROOPS.
FIVE HUNDRED.
CORRECTION.
SIX HUNDRED.
TRAVERSE.
AT MY COMMAND.

When the leader makes an error in the subsequent fire command, he may correct it by announcing CORRECTION, and then repeating the entire subsequent fire command. For example:
LEFT FIVE, DROP ONE.
CORRECTION.
LEFT FIVE, DROP ONE ZERO.

B. Subsequent Fire Commands. If the gunner fails to adjust his fire on the target, the leader must promptly correct him by announcing or signaling the desired changes. When changes are given, the gunner makes the required corrections and continues to engage the target without further command. When firing under the control of a leader, the assistant gunner checks with the leader for instructions, which he passes on to the gunner. Changes in the rate of fire are given orally and by arm-and-hand signals. To interrupt firing, the leader announces CEASE FIRE or gives a signal to cease fire. The gun crew(s) remains on the alert, and firing can be resumed on the same target by announcing FIRE. To terminate the alert, the leader announces CEASE FIRE, END OF MISSION.

Crew Exercises

The purpose of crew exercise is to develop precision, speed, skill, and teamwork in examining equipment, placing the gun into action, and taking it out of action. In crew exercise, precision must be stressed. Once that is attained, speed, skill, and teamwork will follow. Duties are rotated during crew exercise to allow each member of the gun crew to become familiar with all the duties. During crew exercise, all oral or visual signals are repeated. When the fire command is completed, the gunner will give the assistant gunner an UP. The assistant gunner will extend his hand and arm into the air in the direction of the leader (to indicate READY) and announce, UP. With the M3 mount, the crew must consist of at least four men, including the leader. There is no designated crew in the TOE for a dismounted caliber .50 MG. The following paragraphs are only suggestions for the breakdown of equipment and member designation that may be established by the commander.

A. Crew Equipment. In addition to individual arms and equipment, crew members carry the following equipment for the tripod-mounted machine gun:

CREW MEMBER	SUGGESTED MINIMUM EQUIPMENT
Squad or crew leader.	Binoculars, compass, one box of ammunition.
No. 1 Assistant gunner.	Tripod.
No. 2 Gunner.	Receiver, T&E mechanism attached, and headspace and timing gauge.
No. 3 Ammunition bearer.	Barrel, barrel cover, and box of ammunition.

B. Form for Crew Exercise. The crew leader commands, FORM FOR CREW DRILL.

(1) *Positions with equipment.* The crew forms in column, facing the crew leader with five paces between men. They are in the following order: assistant gunner,

gunner, and ammunition bearer. When the crew members reach their correct positions, they assume the prone position with equipment arranged as follows:

(a) No. 1: Tripod to his left, trail legs to the rear, front leg uppermost.

(b) No. 2: Receiver across his front, backplate to the right, retracting slide handle uppermost.

(c) No. 3: Barrel to his right, muzzle to the rear, ammunition box to his left front with latch to the right (latch to the front for the new box).

(d) Other members, if present: Ammunition boxes in front, one foot apart, latches to the right (front).

(e) Crew leader: Ammunition box to his right as he faces the crew, latch to the right (front).

(2) *Rotation of duties.* Duties are rotated to ensure that each member learns and is capable of performing the duties of the other members.

(a) The command to rotate all personnel is, FALL OUT LEADER. At this command, each member of the crew rises, moves forward, and assumes a new duty. The crew leader becomes the ammunition bearer. The assistant gunner moves forward and becomes the crew leader. The gunner moves forward and becomes the assistant gunner. The ammunition bearer moves forward and becomes the gunner.

(b) If the leader is not changed, the command, FALL OUT ASSISTANT GUNNER, is given. At this command, the crew members rise, the gunner becomes the assistant gunner, the ammunition bearer becomes the gunner, and the assistant gunner becomes the ammunition bearer. When the crew members have assumed their new position, they call out their new duties in order, ASSISTANT GUNNER, GUNNER, AMMUNITION BEARER.

NOTE: An additional crew exercise, which the crew may be required to practice, is the setting of headspace and timing. These procedures are outlined in previously.

C. **Inspection of Equipment before Firing.** When the crew is formed with equipment, the command is, INSPECT EQUIPMENT BEFORE FIRING. At this command, the crew proceeds as follows:

(1) The assistant gunner inspects the tripod M3 mount to ensure that:

(a) The indexing levers and clamps on the front and trail legs function properly, and the legs are in the short (low) position.

(b) The front leg and trail legs are closely folded, and the front leg clamp is hand tight.

(c) The sleeve lock latch and pintle lock release cam are in working order, and the pintle lock release cam is down.

(d) The pintle bushing is free from dirt and burrs.

(2) The gunner inspects the receiver group to ensure that:

(a) The barrel support and breech bearing are free of dirt.

(b) The gun pintle is free of dirt.

(c) The feed mechanism and bolt switch are properly assembled to feed from left (soldier raises cover for proper inspection).

(d) The striker projects through the aperture in the face of the bolt (soldier closes the cover).

(e) The rear sight is set at 1,000 yards (900 meters), windage set to zero.

(f) The T&E mechanism is securely attached to the receiver.

(g) The traversing handwheel is centered.

(h) The elevating screws are equally exposed (about 2 inches) above and below elevating handwheel.

(i) The backplate is latched and locked in place.

(j) The bolt-latch release is locked in the down position by the bolt-latch release lock.

(3) The ammunition bearer inspects the barrel and ammunition box to ensure that:

(a) The barrel is clear.

(b) The barrel carrier assembly is securely attached to the barrel.

(c) The barrel threads are free of dirt.

(d) The metallic links are clean (soldier opens ammunition box).

(e) The belt is properly loaded and placed in box with the double-looped end up.

(f) Dummy ammunition is used during crew exercise, and no live ammunition is present.

(g) The box is closed and latched.

(4) When the ammunition bearer completes his inspection, he moves to the gunner's position with the barrel in his right hand and ammunition box in his left hand. With the aid of the gunner, he screws the barrel into the barrel extension. The headspace and timing adjustment is made. The ammunition bearer remains on the left and on line with the gunner.

(5) The crew leader examines his ammunition.

(6) At the completion of the inspection, a report is rendered as follows:

(a) The ammunition bearer reports: AMMUNITION CORRECT (or any deficiencies).

(b) The gunner reports: GUN AND AMMUNITION CORRECT (or any deficiencies).

(c) The assistant gunner reports: ALL CORRECT (or any deficiencies).

D. **Placement of the Gun into Action.** To place the gun into action, the crew leader commands and signals, GUN TO BE MOUNTED HERE (pointing to the position where the gun is to be mounted), FRONT (pointing in the direction of fire), ACTION (vigorously pumping his fist in the direction of the designated gun position).

(1) At the command or signal ACTION, the assistant gunner grasps the left trail leg near the center with his left hand. Springing to his feet and grasping the tripod head with his right hand, he lifts the tripod across the front of his body with the front leg up, and carries the tripod to the desired location. Upon arrival at the position, he places the trail leg pointing upward. Steadying the tripod with his left hand on the front leg, he loosens the front leg clamp with his right hand (Figure 3-42), positions the front leg with his left hand, and tightens the front leg clamp with his right hand. With his right hand on the tripod head, he slides his left hand down on the left trail leg and with a snapping motion, pulls the left leg (to the left), engaging the sleeve latch (Figure 3-43). He then aligns the tripod for direction, drops the mount to the ground, stamps the right and left trail shoes with his right or left foot, and assumes the prone position behind the mount.

Figure 3-42 Assistant gunner- (Number 1) opening the tripod

Figure 3-43 Emplacing the mount

(2) The gunner and ammunition bearer move together (Figure 3-44). When the tripod is nearly mounted, the gunner and ammunition bearer spring to their feet. The gunner places both hands on the spade grips, the ammunition bearer grasps the ammunition box in his left hand and the gun-carrying handle with this right hand. Both men lift the gun from the ground and move rapidly to the gun position. Then the ammunition bearer places the ammunition box on line and in front of the leader's ammunition box. The gunner, assisted by the ammunition bearer, inserts the pintle into the pintle bushing. The ammunition bearer stamps the front shoe into the ground with his left foot, releases the carrying handle, lowers his right hand, and lifts the gun pintle lock release cam. When the gun pintle is fully seated, he presses down the pintle lock release cam with his right hand, turns to his left, and returns to his original position.

Figure 3-44 Mounting the gun

(3) The assistant gunner holds the left spade grip with his left hand. With his right hand, he lowers the T&E mechanism to the traversing bar, ensuring that the traversing handwheel is to the left and the lock lever is to the rear. He then assumes a semi-prone position to the left of the gun with his feet to the rear and his head on line with the feedway. He unlatches and raises the cover of the ammunition box, removes the ammunition belt, inserts the double-looped end into the feedway, and taps the feedway with his right hand to ensure it is closed.

(4) With his right hand palm up, the gunner grasps the retracting slide handle, vigorously jerks it to the rear, and releases it. The gun is half-loaded (Figure 3-45). He then assumes a prone position directly behind the gun with his legs spread and heels down. His right hand lightly grasps the right spade grip with the thumb in position to depress the trigger. His left hand is on the elevating handwheel (palm down) with his thumb near the traversing slide lock lever. He rests on his left elbow with his head as close as possible to the rear sight. He then gives the assistant gunner an UP. The assistant gunner announces UP and extends his hand and arm into the air in the direction of the leader.

Figure 3-45 Gun mounted, gunner half-loading the gun

E. **Removal of the Gun from Action.** To take the gun out of action, the command is OUT OF ACTION.

(1) The gunner raises the cover with his left hand; the assistant gunner lifts the ammunition out of the feedway, replaces the ammunition in the box, and closes and latches the box. The gunner closes the cover, pulls the retracting slide handle to the rear with right hand (palm up) and releases it, presses the trigger with his right thumb, and loosens the traversing slide lock with his left hand. He rises to his feet, grasping both spade grips. At this time, the ammunition bearer will arrive at the gun position. With his left hand, the ammunition bearer grasps the ammunition box and places his right foot on the front leg shoe. With his right hand, he reaches down and lifts up the pintle lock release cam and grasps the carrying handle (Figure 3-46).

Figure 3-46 Crew taking the gun out of action

(2) The gunner and ammunition bearer lift the gun from the tripod, turn right, and carry the gun back to their original position. They set the gun down with the muzzle to the left and the retracting slide handle up. The gunner pulls the retracting slide handle to the rear and aligns the lug on the barrel-locking spring with the 3/8-inch hole in the right side of the receiver. The ammunition bearer unscrews the barrel from the receiver, picks up the ammunition box and barrel, moves five paces to the rear, places the barrel to his right with the muzzle to the rear and the ammunition box to his left, and assumes the prone position.

(3) The gunner rotates the bolt-latch release lock to the right and releases the bolt latch. He checks his sights to ensure they are properly set.

(4) The assistant gunner assumes a kneeling position behind the tripod and releases the sleeve-lock latch with his right hand. He rises to his feet, grasps the front leg with his left hand, and rotates the tripod to a vertical position on the trail

legs. With his right hand, he loosens the front leg clamp, folds down the front leg, and then tightens the clamp. With his right hand on the tripod head, he rotates the tripod on the right trail leg and releases the sleeve latch. Then he folds the left trail leg against the right with his left hand (Figure 3-47). Holding the tripod head with his right hand, trail legs with his left, he lifts the tripod across the front of his body with the front leg up. He turns to the right and returns to his original position. At this time, the crew leader picks up his ammunition box and faces the crew. The assistant gunner places the tripod on the ground, assumes a prone position to the right of the tripod, and announces UP.

Figure 3-47 Folding the trail legs

F. **Duties of The Crew.** To hand-carry the gun and equipment, the command is SECURE EQUIPMENT, FOLLOW ME. At this command,

(1) The crew leader carries his ammunition box in his right hand.

(2) The assistant gunner carries the tripod over either shoulder.

(3) The gunner carries the receiver on either shoulder with the spade grips to the front.

(4) The ammunition bearer carries his ammunition box in his left hand and the barrel in his right hand with the muzzle to the rear (or on his left shoulder with the muzzle to the front).

G. **Relocation of Tripod-mounted Gun.** When the gun is mounted on the tripod, it can be moved for short distances by dragging or by a two- or three-man carry. (In the latter, the men should move in step to make carrying easier.)

(1) *Dragging.* The gun is dragged when there is limited cover, or when the situation requires the gun to be moved in this manner. The gunner and assistant gunner drag the mounted gun to the desired position (Figure 3-48).

Figure 3-48 Dragging the gun into position

(2) *Two-man carry.* With the gunner on the right and assistant gunner on the left, each grasps the front leg with his forward hand and a trail leg with the other hand, just above the traversing bar (Figure 3-49).

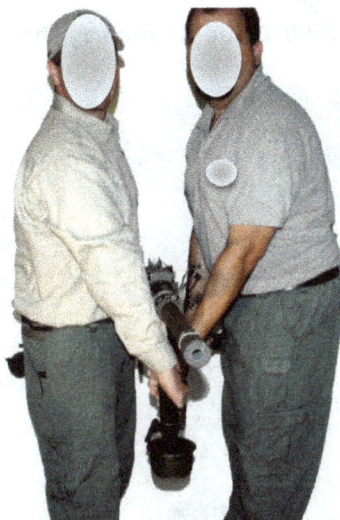

Figure 3-49 Two-man carry

(3) *Three-man carry.* When the barrel is hot, the gunner gets behind the tripod with a trail leg in each hand. With the assistant gunner on the left and the ammunition bearer on the right, each grasps the carrying handle. In addition, the assistant gunner carries the ammunition in his left hand (Figure 3-50). When the barrel is cool, the ammunition bearer and the assistant gunner each grasp the front leg (Figure 3-51).

Figure 3-50 Three-man carry (hot barrel)

Figure 3-51 Three-man carry (cold barrel)

NOTE: Carrying the gun by the barrel may cause damage to the barrel support and the barrel extension.

H. **Movement of the Gun to Other Mounts.** With the mount prepared to receive the gun, the cradle of the mount is placed in a horizontal position. To move the gun to the mount, the gunner carries the right spade grip in his left hand and a box of ammunition in his right. The assistant gunner grasps the carrying handle with his left hand and a box of ammunition in his right hand. When they get to the mount, the gunner and assistant gunner place their ammunition boxes near the mount. The gunner removes the rear mounting (gun-locking) pin with his right hand. The assistant gunner removes the front mounting (gun-locking) pin with his right hand. They place the gun on the mount. The gunner aligns the holes in the rear mounting lugs of the receiver with the rear mounting bracket and inserts the rear mounting pin. The assistant gunner aligns the front mounting hole in the front of the receiver with the front mounting bracket and inserts the front mounting pin. (For use of the side plate trigger with the M63 mount, see TM 9-1005-213-10.)

Machine Gun Fundamental Skills Test

The machine gun fundamental skills test should be held periodically to ensure that proficiency with the MG is maintained by all crewmen. It consists of 10 fundamental skills; all tasks are hands-on. The test should be given prior to range firing on a go/no-go basis.

TASK	GO/NO GO
1. Clear the MG.	
2. Disassemble the MG.	
3. Assemble the MG.	
4. Conduct a function check.	
5. Maintain the MG.	
6. Set the headspace on the MG.	
7. Set the timing on the MG.	
8. Load the MG.	
9. Perform immediate action on the MG.	
10. Unload the MG.	

Sights

Windage adjustments: For minor adjustments left and right, you can use the deflection wheel on the cradle; for major adjustments, loosen the locking ring on the cradle and tripod mating platform, point the weapon, and then retighten when oriented correctly.

Elevation adjustments: For minor adjustments up and down, you can use the elevation wheel on the cradle; for major adjustments, loosen the locking lever on the cradle, point the weapon, and then retighten when oriented correctly.

Front and Rear Sight

Figure 3-52a Rear Tangent Sight

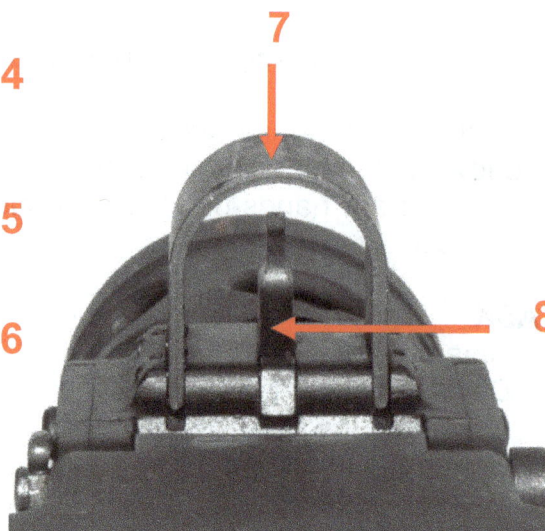

Figure 3-52b Front Sight

1 – Windage Knob
2 – Mils
3 – Range in Yards and Mils
4 – Elevating screw knob

5 – Yards
6 – Deflection in Mils
7 – Cover
8 - Blade

Sighting

A. <u>Sight alignment</u>. The gunner will center the front sight blade in the aperture of the rear sight, with the top of the sight blade centered in the rear sight aperture (Figure 3-53).

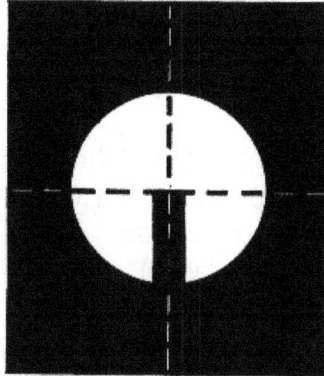

Figure 3-53 Proper sight alignment

B. <u>Sight picture</u>. The gunner will maintain correct sight alignment on the center base (6 o'clock) of the target so it appears to rest on the top of the front sight blade (Figure 3-54).

Figure 3-50 Proper sight picture

C. <u>Duties of the gunner and assistant gunner/team leader while sighting</u>. When the squad leader announces the range to the target, the assistant gunner/team leader will raise the rear sight and apply the appropriate range setting. Once the gunner has acquired the target, he will announce, **"SIGHTED."** At this time, the assistant gunner/team leader lowers the rear sight and announces, **"GUN UP."**

Concept of Zeroing/Targeting

The concept of zero is very simple; it is no more than the best way to adjust the sights of the weapon so the point of aim of the sights and the point of impact of the rounds are the same at any given range. A properly zeroed M2 gives the gunner the highest probability of hit for most combat targets with the least adjustment to the point of aim. There are three methods of zeroing/targeting used with the .50 caliber MG.

A. Ten-meter zero is the basic and the most common method of zeroing the M2 MG. Once zeroed on a 10-meter range using the standard machine-gun target, the weapon is ready for field fire. As with other weapons, the sight on the M2 must also be set at an initial start point. The initial sight setting for field zero is basically the same, except the range setting during field zero will depend on the range to the target, and it is always 1,000 yards for 10 meters.

(1) *Set elevation.* Raise the rear sight by lifting straight up until it snaps into the upright position. Adjust the range scale to 1,000 yards by rotating the elevation screw knob in the necessary direction. (Clockwise moves the scale up; counterclockwise moves the scale down.)

(2) *Set windage.* Rotate the windage knob until the zero index mark on the base rear sight is aligned with the index mark on the top of the receiver. (Clockwise moves the windage scale to the left; counterclockwise moves it to the right.)

Loading the .50 BMG

Trainers must ensure that the weapon functions correctly and that proper headspace and timing have been set before loading. When loading in either mode, the ammunition is fed into the MG in the same manner (Figures 3-55a & 3-55b). Ensure that the bolt is forward and the cover is closed. Insert the double-loop end of the ammunition belt into the feed way until the first round is engaged by the belt-holding pawl. Figures 3-55a & 3-55b shows the correct position of the bolt latch in the single-shot or automatic mode.

Methods of Engagement

A. **Single-shot Mode**. When engaging targets at ranges greater than 1,100 meters, using the single-shot mode (firing one round at a time) allows the gunner to deliver well-aimed fire on the target. To load in the single-shot mode
(1) Keep the bolt-latch release unlocked in the up position, and release it manually for each round.
(2) Jerk the retracting slide handle to the rear and lock it in position. Return the retracting slide handle to the forward position and then release the bolt by pressing the bolt-latch release. The gun is now half-loaded.
(3) To complete loading, jerk the retracting slide handle to the rear and lock it in position. Return the retracting slide handle to the forward position. Press the bolt latch release. When the bolt goes forward for the second time, the gun is loaded.

B. **Automatic Mode**. To load in the automatic mode
(1) Lock the bolt-latch release down with the bolt-latch release lock.
(2) Jerk the retracting slide handle to the rear and release it. The gun is now half-loaded.
(3) To complete loading, jerk the retracting slide handle to the rear a second time and release it. When the bolt goes forward for the second time, the gun is loaded.

Rear View   **Side View**
Figure 3-55a Firing mode (single shot)

Rear View   Side View

Figure 3-55b Firing mode (automatic fire)

Loading, Cover Raised

A. Ensure that the bolt is in the forward position.

B. Insert the double-loop end of the ammunition into the feed-way over the belt-holding pawl (Figure 3-56a) and press the extractor down into position to extract the round from the link (Figure 3-56b).

Figure 3-56a Double link up to the cartridge down

Figure 3-56b Pressing the extractor stop

C. Close the cover.

D. Pull the retracting slide handle to the rear and release it (Figure 3-57a). If the weapon is in automatic mode, the bolt and retracting slide handle will move forward under pressure of the driving spring rod assembly, but if in single-shot mode, the retracting slide handle must be returned forward and the bolt-latch release must be pressed to allow the bolt to go forward (Figure 3-57b). Repeat this step one more time for a full load.

Figure 3-57a Retracting the bolt

Figure 3-57b Releasing the bolt forward

Loading, Cover Closed

A. Ensure that the bolt is in the forward position.

B. Close the cover.

C. Insert the double-loop end of the ammunition into the feed-way until the belt-holding pawl engages the first round (Figure 3-58).

Figure 3-58 Inserting ammunition into the feed way

D. Pull the retracting slide handle to the rear and release it (Figure 3-59a). If the weapon is in automatic mode, the bolt and retracting slide handle will move forward under pressure of the driving spring rod assembly, but if in single-shot mode, the retracting slide handle must be returned forward and the bolt-latch release must be pressed to allow the bolt to go forward (Figure 3-59b). Repeat this step one more time for a full load.

Figure 3-59a Retracting the bolt

Figure 3-59b Releasing the bolt forward

Unloading the .50 BMG

To unload the MG, the gunner must first ensure that the weapon is in the single-shot mode. The cover is then lifted, and the assistant gunner removes the ammunition belt from the feed way, and the bolt is locked to the rear. If a round is chambered, it will release, unfired, when the bolt locks to the rear. Once the bolt is locked to the rear, the chamber and T-slot are examined to ensure that they are not holding rounds. In darkness, this action must be done by feeling the areas. After the examination has been done (during training), a wooden block is inserted in the receiver between the bolt and the rear of the barrel, extending above and below the receiver about one inch. Then a cleaning rod is inserted in the muzzle end of the barrel and pushed through the bore until it can be seen in the receiver. Remove the rod; the gun is now clear (Figure 3-60).

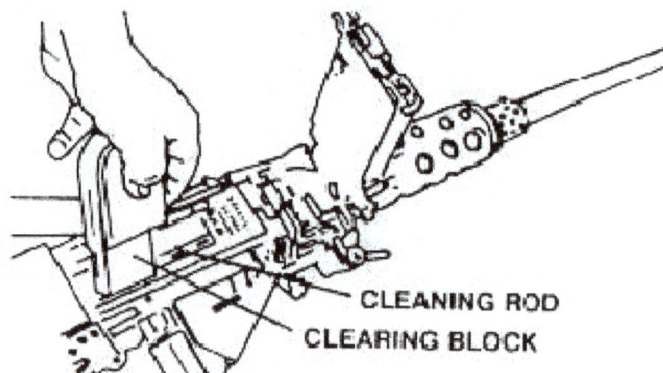

Figure 3-60 The clearing block

Firing the .50 BMG

Orient toward the desired area/target, take a proper sight alignment and sight picture, ensure you are set on the desired mode of fire (single or full auto), and depress the trigger butterfly. You should maintain a 6-to 9-round burst for control and avoid the overheating of the barrel when possible. Firing more than 200 rounds continuously will increase the possibility of cook offs (the heat of the barrel is so great that it ignites the powder in the unchambered round).

ENGAGE TARGETS. To engage targets effectively, you will need to know how to employ the gun using the tripod with proper body position.

The traversing and elevating (T&E) mechanism permits controlled manipulation in both direction and elevation and makes it possible to engage predetermined targets during darkness or periods of reduced visibility.

Trigger Manipulation

- Push (not squeeze) the trigger down (quick and hard) and then release (quickly). The weapon can be damaged by not pulling the trigger to the rear quickly and not releasing quickly when firing.

- Bursts of less than 6 rounds should not be fired.

- The rapid rate of fire of 200 rounds per minute is delivered in bursts of 10 to 12 rounds, which are fired 2 to 3 seconds apart.

- The sustained rate of fire of 100 rounds per minute is delivered in bursts of 6 to 8 rounds, which are fired 4 to 5 seconds apart.

Position and Grip on Tripod-Mounted Gun

A. Prone Position

(1) The gunner assumes the prone position behind the gun.

(2) The legs will be spread at a comfortable distance apart with the heels down, if possible.

(3) The right hand will grasp the spade grip with the thumb off the trigger until ready to fire. A firm shoulder pressure to the right and down will be applied.

(4) The left hand will be placed against the left spade grip palm open, applying rightward shoulder pressure.

(5) In order to fire a tight group, the gunner must maintain his position and grip with a consistent amount of right and down shoulder pressure during firing.

B. Sitting Position

(1) The gunner sits directly behind the gun. He will cross his legs.

(2) The gunner places his elbows inside his thighs to obtain maximum support.

(3) The right hand will grasp the spade grip with the thumb off the trigger until ready to fire. A firm shoulder pressure to the right and down will be applied.

(4) The left hand will be placed on the left spade grip palm open, applying rightward shoulder pressure.

C. Standing Position

(1) The gunner stands directly behind the weapon with his feet approximately shoulder width apart.

(2) The elbows are tucked firmly to the gunner's side, and the gunner will lean slightly into the weapon.

(3) The right hand will grasp the spade grip with the thumb off the trigger until ready to fire. A firm shoulder pressure to the right and down will be applied.

(4) The left hand will be placed on the left spade grip palm open, applying rightward shoulder pressure.

Manipulation Procedures

A. All manipulations of the traversing and elevating mechanism are made with the left hand.

B. Changes in direction will always be made first, then changes in elevation.

C. The six manipulations used with the tripod-mounted M2 heavy machine gun are fixed, traversing, search, traverse and search, swinging traverse, and free gun.

(1) Fixed Fire. Fixed fire requires no adjustment of the T&E once the weapon is on target.

(2) Traversing Adjustment

(a) To move the muzzle of the gun to the right, the gunner places his left hand on the traversing hand wheel, thumb up, and pushes with his thumb away from himself (Push right).

(b) To move the muzzle left, the gunner will pull his thumb towards himself (Pull-left).

(3) <u>Searching Adjustment</u>

(a) To move the muzzle of the gun up, the gunner will grasp the elevating hand wheel with his left palm down and push his thumb away from himself (push-up).

(b) To move the muzzle of the gun down, the gunner will grasp the elevating hand wheel with his left palm down and pull his thumb towards himself (pull-down).

(4) <u>Traverse and Search Adjustment</u>. Traverse and Search adjustment is a combination of the previous two methods. The traverse is done first, followed by the search.

(5) <u>Swinging Traverse</u>. Swinging Traverse adjustment is utilized on targets requiring large, rapid changes in direction but little or no changes in elevation. The gunner loosens the slide lock lever enough to move the T&E freely across the traversing bar. With his palm on the slide lock lever and his fingers grasping the elevating hand wheel, the gunner makes direction changes by sliding the traversing slide across the traversing bar.

(6) <u>Free gun</u>. Fire delivered against moving targets, which must be quickly engaged and which require rapid changes in both direction and elevation. Examples are aerial, vehicles, mounted troops, or infantry in close formation moving rapidly toward or away from the gun position.

Destruction Procedures

The decision to destroy the gun to prevent its capture and use by the enemy is a command decision. It will be ordered and carried out only on authority delegated by the major unit commander.

- Destroy the machine gun and mount only when they are subject to capture or abandonment. Destruction must be as complete as circumstances permit.
- Lacking time for complete destruction, destroy the parts essential to operation of the gun, beginning with those parts most difficult for the enemy to duplicate.
- Destroy the same parts of each gun to prevent the reconstruction of a complete gun from several damaged guns.

The following methods may be used to destroy specific components of the BMG.

A. Gun. Field strip the gun. Use the barrel as a sledge. Raise the cover and smash the cover forward and down toward the barrel support. Smash the backplate group. Remove the firing pin from the bolt; place the striker in the hole in the face of the bolt and bend it until broken. Remove the barrel buffer-tube lock assembly from the barrel buffer body group and bend and deform it. Smash and bend the breech lock depressors. Place the barrel extension in the rear of the receiver with the barrel extension shank protruding; knock off the shank by striking it with the barrel from the side. Deform and crack the receiver by striking it with the barrel at the side plate corners nearest the feed way. Smash the extractor.

B. Tripod Mount, M3. Leave the pintle on the tripod by removing the pintle bolt from the gun. Use the barrel as a sledge. Strike the sides of the pintle and deform it. Fold the trail legs and turn the mount over. Stand on the folded trail legs and knock off the pintle latch (pintle lock-release cam). Smash the elevating mechanism with the barrel. If possible, smash the rear legs to prevent unfolding.

C. Anti-aircraft Mount, M63. Remove the side plate trigger control mechanism from its container or the gun, and deform it by using the barrel. Lock the cradle and yoke assembly in the horizontal position and beat the trigger frame assembly and cradle until they are bent down along the elevator assembly. Strike the elevator from the side with the barrel until it is bent so that the elevator will not rotate in the base.

D. Spare Parts. Destroy the bolt, barrel extension, firing pins, and barrel buffer groups. Break or deform all other parts.

E. Ammunition. When time permits and material is available, destroy ammunition by burning. Unpack all ammunition from boxes or cartons, stack the ammunition in a heap and, using flammable material available, ignite and take cover immediately.

F. Burning. To destroy the gun by burning, place a thermite grenade in the receiver on the bolt (with the cover resting on the grenade) and fire the grenade. (This method may require the use of more than one grenade.) Remove the backplate group, place a thermite grenade in the rear of the receiver and fire the grenade.

G. Disposal. Bury in suitable holes, or dump parts into streams, mud, snow, sumps, and latrines, or scatter the parts over a wide area.

Section 4

Performance Problems

Malfunction and Immediate Action Procedures

Malfunctions are usually preventable through good practices, but they may still occur out of the blue from time to time. Of course, you hope it is on the practice range, but you should treat each one as if you are in a life-or-death situation. Practicing proper and effective corrective actions will allow you to be more confident in your weapon handling. In stressful situations, you can become much more stressed due to an unforeseen malfunction that can be dealt with easily.

Proper training will do more to save your life than technology. Malfunction drills must fix the problem 100% of the time (excluding a weapon stoppage—broken weapon) the first time performed. You must look at the weapon and identify the problem (obviously the weapon is not functioning as you need it to, so you must transition to another weapon or rectify the situation). It is a non-functioning weapon at this point—fix it.

A malfunction is any failure of the gun to function satisfactorily. Examples of malfunctions are:

a. Failure to Function Freely. Sluggish operation is usually due to human failure to eliminate excessive friction caused by dirt, lack of proper lubrication, burred parts, incorrect headspace adjustment, or incorrect timing.

b. Uncontrolled Automatic Fire. Uncontrolled automatic fire (runaway gun) occurs when fire continues even when the trigger or trigger control mechanism is released. If the cause is present before the gun is fired, the gun will start to fire when the recoiling groups move into battery the second time. If the defect occurs during firing, the gun will continue firing when the trigger control mechanism is released. A runaway gun may be caused –
 • By a bent trigger lever, forward end of the trigger lever sprung downward.
 • By burred beveled contacting surfaces of the trigger lever and sear.
 • By a jammed or broken side plate trigger.

To stop the uncontrolled automatic fire:
(1) Keep the gun laid on target.
(2) Twist the belt, causing the gun to jam.
(3) Caution, do not unlatch the cover.
(4) Wait 5 minutes to guard against cook off.
(5) Clear weapon, replace broken, worn, or burred parts. Check the side plate trigger and trigger control mechanism, when applicable.

Stoppages

A stoppage is any interruption in the cycle of operation caused by the faulty action of the gun or ammunition. Stoppages are classified as follows:

A. Failure to Feed. Prevents the round from being properly positioned in the receiver group.

B. Failure to Chamber. Prevents the complete chambering of the round.

C. Failure to Lock. Prevents the breech lock from correctly entering its recess in the bolt.

D. Failure to Fire. Prevents the ignition of the round.

E. Failure to Unlock. Prevents the breech lock from moving out of its recess in the bolt.

F. Failure to Extract. Prevents the extraction of the expended cartridge from the chamber.

G. Failure to Eject. Prevents the ejection of the expended cartridge from the receiver.

H. Failure to Cock. Prevents the firing pin extension from being engaged with the sear.

Stoppages and Their Causes

NATURE OF STOPPAGE	USUAL CAUSES	OTHER CAUSES
Failure to feed.	Defective ammunition belt. Defective feed mechanism. Defective extractor.	Improperly loaded belt. Short round.
Failure to chamber.	Broken part or obstruction in T-slot or chamber. Separated (ruptured) case.	Thick or thin rim, bulged round, protruding primer.
Failure to lock.	Incorrect headspace.	Broken parts. Battered breech lock. Battered breech lock cam. Faulty breech lock cam adjustment.

Failure to fire.	Defective parts in firing mechanism. Defective ammunition. Incorrect timing.	
Failure to unlock.	Broken parts in receiver.	Worn or faulty breech lock cam, or faulty adjustment.
Failure to extract.	Dirty chamber.	Defective cartridge case.
Failure to eject.	Defective ejector.	Burred T-slot.
Failure to cock.	Broken sear. Worn sear notch. Weak sear spring. Worn hooked notch on firing pin extension.	Broken cocking lever.

Immediate Action

Immediate action is the first thing to be done by the operator when a stoppage to reduce a stoppage.

Immediate action is performed by the gunner; however, every crewmember must be trained to apply immediate action. The following procedures will assist in reducing most stoppages without analyzing their causes in detail.

WARNING
Failure to follow procedures may result in damage to weapon and injury to personnel.

A. If gun fails to fire, take the following action:

(1) Wait 5 seconds; a hangfire maybe causing the misfire. In the next 5 seconds, pull the bolt to the rear (check for ejection and feeding of belt), release it, re-lay on the target, and attempt to fire. If the bolt-latch release and trigger are depressed at the same time, the bolt goes forward and the weapon should fire automatically.

(2) If the gun again fails to fire, wait 5 seconds, pull the bolt to the rear (engage with bolt latch if applicable), and return the retracting slide handle to its forward position. Open the cover and remove the belted ammunition. Inspect the gun to determine the cause of stoppage.

B. A hangfire or cook-off can cause injury to personnel or damage to the weapon. To avoid these, the gunner must take the following precautions:

(1) Always keep the round locked in the chamber the first 5 seconds after a misfire occurs. This prevents an explosion outside of the gun in event of a hangfire.

(2) If the barrel is hot, the round must be extracted within the next 5 seconds to prevent a cook-off. When more than 150 rounds have been fired in a 2-minute period, the barrel is hot enough to produce a cook-off.

3) If the barrel is hot and the round cannot be extracted within the 10 seconds, it must remain locked in the chamber for at least 5 minutes, to guard against a cook-off.

(4) Keep the gun cover closed during the waiting periods.

Remedial Action

When immediate action does not correct the malfunction, the quickest way to resume firing is to replace the defective part.

A. Removal of a Cartridge from the T-Slot. If the cartridge does not fall out, hold the bolt to the rear, and with the extractor raised, use a screwdriver to push the cartridge out the bottom of the receiver.

B. Removal of a Ruptured Cartridge. A ruptured (separated) cartridge case may be removed with a cleaning rod or ruptured cartridge extractor. When using the ruptured cartridge extractor, raise the cover and pull the bolt to the rear. Place the extractor in the T-slot of the bolt in the same manner as that of a cartridge, so that it is held in line with the bore by the ejector of the extractor assembly of the gun. With the extractor aligned with the bore and held firmly in the T-slot, let the bolt go forward into the ruptured case, and the shoulders will spring out in front of the case. Pull the bolt to the rear and remove the ruptured case and extractor (Figures 4-1 and 4-2).

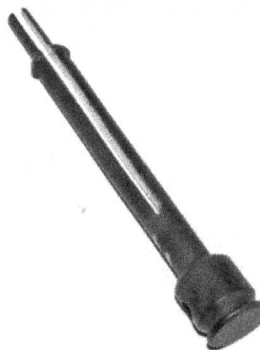

Figure 4-1 The ruptured cartridge case extractor

Figure 4-2. Ruptured cartridge case extractor aligned with the chamber

REFERENCES:

- TM 02498A-10/1 *Operator's Manual Machineguns, Caliber .50, Browning M2 Heavy Barrel.*
- FM 23-65 *Browning Machinegun Caliber .50 HB M2.*
- Gresham, John D. *"Weapons." Military Heritage.* December 2001. Volume 3, No. 3: 22- 30 (John Browning's (M2) .50-caliber).
- MCWP 3-15.1: *Machine Guns and Machine Gun Gunnery.*

Appendix A- Ammunition

WARNING- Inspect all cartridges for uniformity, cleanliness, and serviceability. Check all for undented primers, and only use issued ammunition.

The **.50 Browning Machine Gun** (12.7×99mm NATO) or **.50 BMG** is a cartridge developed for the Browning .50 Caliber machine gun in the late 1910s. Entering service officially in 1921, the round is based on a scaled-up .30-06 cartridge. The cartridge itself has been made in many variants: multiple generations of regular ball, tracer, armor-piercing (AP), incendiary, and saboted sub-caliber rounds. The rounds intended for machine guns are linked using metallic links.

The .50 BMG cartridge is also used in long-range target and sniper rifles, as well as other .50 machine guns. The use in single-shot and semi-automatic rifles has resulted in many specialized match-grade rounds not used in .50 machine guns.

A wide variety of ammunition is available; the availability of match-grade ammunition has increased the usefulness of .50 caliber rifles by allowing more accurate fire than lower-quality rounds.

The round was conceptualized during WWI by John Browning in response to a requirement for an anti-aircraft weapon. The round itself is based on a scaled-up .30-06 Springfield design, and the machine gun was based on a scaled-up M1919/M1917 design that Browning had initially developed at the turn of century (but which was not adopted by the U.S. military until 1917, hence the model designation). The new heavy machine gun, the Browning M2 .50 caliber machine gun, was used heavily in aircraft, especially during World War II, though its airborne use is limited to helicopters at present. It was and still is used on the ground as well, both vehicle mounted, in fixed fortifications, and on occasion, carried by infantry. The incendiary rounds were especially good against aircraft, and the AP rounds were good for destroying concrete bunkers, structures, and lighter armored fighting vehicles.

The development of the .50 round is sometimes confused with the German 13mm TuF, which was developed by Germany for an anti-tank rifle to combat British tanks during WWI. However, the development of the U.S. .50 round was started before this later German project was completed or even known to the Allied countries. When word of the German anti-tank round spread, there was some debate as to whether it should be copied and used as a base for the new machine gun cartridge. However, after some analysis, the German ammunition was ruled out, both because performance was inferior to the modified Springfield .30-06 round and because it was a semi-rimmed cartridge, making it sub-optimal for an automatic weapon. The round's dimensions and ballistic traits are different. The M2 would, however, go on to function as an anti-armor machine gun, and decades later, be used in high-powered rifles. The concept of a .50 machine gun was not an invention of this era; this caliber (.50) had been used in Maxim machine guns and in a number of manual machine guns, such as the Gatling.

During World War II, it found use in penetrating lightly armored vehicles, including aircraft. An upgraded variant of the Browning machine gun used during World War II is still in use today as the well-known M2 machine gun. Since the mid-1950s, some armored personnel carriers and utility vehicles have been made to withstand 12.7mm machine gun fire, thus making it a much less flexible weapon. It still has more penetrating power than light machine guns, such as general purpose machine guns, but is difficult to maintain and aim in field conditions. Its range and accuracy, however, are superior to light machine guns when fixed and water cooled, and it has not been replaced as the standard caliber for western vehicle-mounted machine guns (Soviet and CIS armored vehicles mount 12.7mm DShK, NSV, which are ballistically very similar to the .50 BMG, or 14.5mm KPV machine guns, which have significantly superior armor penetration compared to any 12.7mm round).

The Barrett M82 .50 Caliber rifle and later variants were born during the 1980s and have upgraded the anti-material power of the military sniper. A skilled sniper can effectively neutralize an infantry unit by picking off several soldiers at a very long range, without revealing his precise location, then spend a few hours moving to a new position (while the infantry unit decides to hunt down the sniper or to retreat) before firing again. However, due to the great destructive power of the ammunition, such heavy-caliber sniper rifles are considered anti-material weapons.

The round is different from the one used in the Boys anti-tank rifle, developed in the 1930s in Britain, which used a belted design and a slightly larger-diameter bullet, .55 Boys (13.9x99B).

The caliber .50 cartridge consists of a cartridge case, primer, propelling charge, and the bullet. The term bullet refers only to the small-arms projectile. There are eight types of ammunition issued for use in the caliber .50 machine gun. The tips of the various rounds are color-coded to indicate their type. The ammunition is linked with the M2 or M9 metallic links for use in the machine gun (Figure A-1).

Figure A-1 4:1 Link

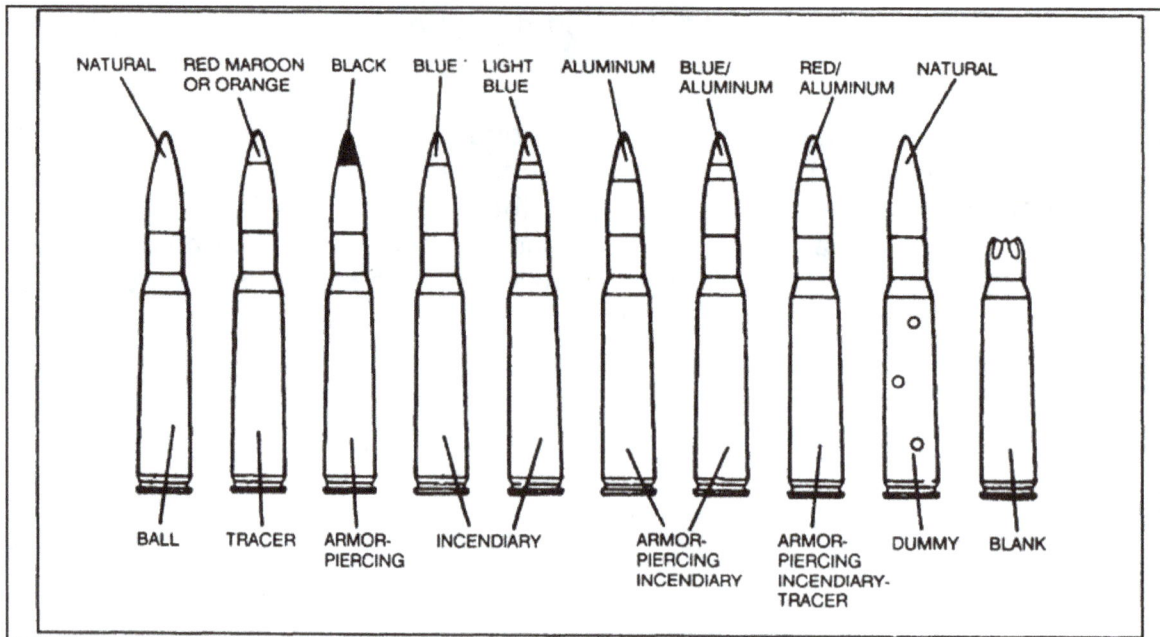
Figure A-2 Various .50 BMG Cartridges

Types of Ammunition (Figure A-2)

A. <u>M2 or M33 Ball Cartridge</u>. The M2 ball cartridge is for use in marksmanship training, against personnel and light material targets. It is identified by the solid bronze tip with no other markings.

B. <u>Tracer Cartridge M1, M10, M17, M20</u>. The tracer cartridge is to aid in observing fire. Secondary purposes are for incendiary effect and for signaling. It is identified by a red or brown tip.

C. <u>M2 Armor-Piercing Cartridge</u>. The M2 armor-piercing cartridge is for use against armored aircraft and lightly armored vehicles, concrete shelters, bunkers, and other bullet-resisting targets. It is identified by a black tip.

D. <u>MI Incendiary Cartridge</u>. The MI incendiary cartridge is used for producing incendiary effects, especially against aircraft. It is identified by a blue tip.

E. <u>M8 Armor-Piercing Incendiary Cartridge</u>. The M8 armor-piercing incendiary cartridge is used for combined armor piercing and incendiary effect. It is identified by an aluminum tip or blue tip with an aluminum ring.

F. <u>M20 Armor-Piercing Incendiary Tracer Cartridge</u>. The M20 armor- piercing incendiary tracer is used for combined armor piercing and incendiary effects with the additional tracer feature. It is identified by a red tip with an aluminum ring.

G. <u>M903 Sabot Light Armor Penetrator Cartridge</u>. The M903 sabot light armor penetrator is used against light armored vehicles and aircraft. Also called SLAP. It is identified by its tungsten penetrator in an amber-tinted sabot.

H. <u>M962 Sabot Light Armor Penetrator Tracer Cartridge</u>. The sabot light armor penetrator-tracer is for use against light armored vehicles and aircraft with the additional tracer feature. Also called SLAP-T. It is identified by its tungsten penetrator in a red-tinted sabot.

I. <u>M1AI Blank Cartridge</u>. The M1A1 blank cartridge is used for simulated firing. It is identified by the lack of a projectile.

J. <u>M858 Ball, Plastic Practice</u>. The M858 ball, plastic practice round is used in scaled-down range training, for example, where range restrictions limit or prohibit use of one of the other types of live ammunition. It is identified by its blue plastic bullet and case.

K. <u>M680 Tracer Plastic Practice</u>. The M680 tracer plastic practice is used with the ball plastic practice on scaled-down ranges. It is identified by its blue plastic bullet with red tip and plastic case.

L. <u>M2 Dummy Cartridge</u>. This cartridge is used for crew drill and practice in loading and unloading the gun. It is identified by the three holes drilled in the cartridge case and the lack of primer.

Ammunition Precautions

A. Ammunition containers should not be opened until you are ready to use them.

B. You should protect the ammunition from mud, dirt, and water. If the ammunition gets dirty or corroded, it must be cleaned before firing.

C. Do not expose ammunition to the direct rays of the sun for long periods of time.

D. Do not oil or grease ammunition, as it will collect dirt.

E. Replace any defective ammunition when you check it prior to firing.

F. Any ammunition marked **"FOR TRAINING PURPOSE ONLY"** is not to be fired over the heads of friendly troops.

Ammunition Packing

- M2 .50 cal. ammunition comes in a metal can.
- Each can contain 100 rounds.
- Ball ammunition normally comes linked with a ratio of one tracer to every four ball rounds.
- Ammunition is issued in a disintegrating, metallic, split-linked belt.

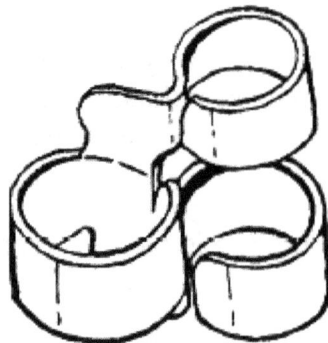

.50 Caliber M2 Link   .50 Caliber M9 Link

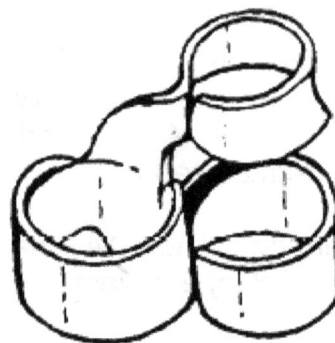

Ballistic Data. The approximate maximum range and average muzzle velocity of some of the different types of caliber .50 ammunition authorized for use in the machine gun are noted below.

Ballistic Data, U.S. Military Cartridges

CARTRIDGE	MAX RANGE (M)	METER TRACE	AVERAGE MUZZLE VEL. (FPS)
Ball, M2	7,400	N/A	2,930
Tracer, M1 (gliding metal jacket)	5,575	1,800	2,860
Tracer, M1 (clad steel jacket)	5,450	1,800	3,030
Tracer, M17	5,450	2,450	3,030
Incendiary, M1	6,050	N/A	3,090
Armor-piercing, M2	7,400	N/A	2,930
Armor-piercing-Incendiary, M8	6,470	N/A	3,050
Armor-piercing-Incendiary-tracer, M20	6,470	*300-1,750	3,050

* This tracer is dim at near ranges but increases to bright as it moves farther from the gun.

Care, Handling, and Preservation. Exercise care to prevent ammunition boxes from becoming broken or damaged. If they do, repair them immediately. Transfer all original markings to the new parts of the box. Do not open ammunition boxes until the ammunition is to be used. Ammunition removed from the airtight container, particularly in damp climates, is likely to corrode. Protect the ammunition from mud, sand, and water. If the ammunition gets wet or dirty, wipe it off at once with a clean, dry cloth. Wipe off light corrosion as soon as it is discovered. Turn in heavily corroded cartridges. Do not expose ammunition to the direct rays of the sun. If the powder is hot, excessive pressure may be developed when the weapon is fired. Do not oil or grease ammunition. Dust and
other abrasives that collect on greasy ammunition are injurious to the operating parts of the gun. Moreover, oiled cartridges produce excessive chamber pressure. Do not fire dented cartridges, cartridges with loose bullets, or otherwise defective rounds.

Storage. Small-arms ammunition is not an explosive hazard, but under poor storage conditions, it may become a fire hazard. Store ammunition of all classes away from radiators, hot-water pipes, and other sources of heat. Whenever possible, store ammunition under cover. If it is necessary to leave ammunition in the open, keep it at least 6 inches off the ground and covered with a double thickness of tarpaulin. Place the tarpaulin so that it gives maximum protection and allows free circulation of air. Dig suitable trenches to prevent water from flowing under the ammunition pile.

Miscellaneous Data. Table A-1 lists the maximum penetration in inches for an armor-piercing cartridge fired from the 45-inch barrel (muzzle velocity, 2,935 feet per second), which in some cases may enhance the leader's selection of targets to engage.

	INCHES AT:		
MATERIAL	200 METERS	600 METERS	1,500 METERS
Armor plate (homogeneous)	1.0	0.7	0.3
Armor plate (face-hardened)	0.9	0.5	0.2
Sand (100 pounds dry weight/cubic feet)	14.0	12.0	16.0
Clay (100 pounds dry weight/cubic feet)	28.0	27.0	21.0

Table A-1 Maximum penetration for armor-piercing cartridge

Table A-2 lists the maximum penetration in inches for a ball cartridge fired from the 45-inch barrel (muzzle velocity, 2,935 feet per second).

	INCHES AT:		
MATERIAL	200 M	600 M	1,500 M
Sand (100 pounds dry weight)	14.0	12.0	6.0
Clay (100 pounds dry weight)	28.0	27.0	21.0
Concrete	2.0	1.0	1.0

Table A-2 Maximum penetration for ball cartridge

Appendix B – Ammunition Comparison

9x18mm Makarov   9x19mm Luger   7.62x25mm Tokarev   .45 ACP

Pistols and Submachine Guns

NATO & SOVIET BLOC AMMUNITION COMPARISON

5.56x 45mm   5.45x 39mm   5.56x 45mm   7.62x 39mm   7.62x 51mm   7.62x 54R mm   12.7x99mm (.50 BMG)   12.7x108mm

Assault Rifles   Sniper Rifles and Machine Guns

www.ingramcontent.com/pod-product-compliance
Lightning Source LLC
Chambersburg PA
CBHW080517110426
42742CB00017B/3152